teach yourself®

guitar

teach yourself ®

guitar
dale fradd

For over 60 years, more than
40 million people have learnt over
750 subjects the **teach yourself**
way, with impressive results.

be where you want to be
with **teach yourself**

Dedication

In memory of my parents who loved the sound of the guitar and who always encouraged me to make music.

Acknowledgements

For permission to reproduce copyright material in this book, the author and publishers are grateful to Oxford University Press for two extracts from *Partita* by Stephen Dodgson, and to Editions Max Eschig for extracts from *Prélude 1, Prélude 2,* and *Prélude 4* by Villa-Lobos.

For UK order enquiries: please contact Bookpoint Ltd, 130 Milton Park, Abingdon, Oxon OX14 4SB. Telephone: (44) 01235 827720. Fax: (44) 01235 400454. Lines are open from 09.00–18.00, Monday to Saturday, with a 24-hour message answering service. Details about our titles and how to order are available at www.teachyourself.co.uk

For USA order enquiries: please contact McGraw-Hill Customer Services, PO Box 545, Blacklick, OH 43004-0545, USA. Telephone: 1-800-722-4726. Fax: 1-614-755-5645.

For Canada order enquiries: please contact McGraw-Hill Ryerson Ltd, 300 Water St, Whitby, Ontario L1N 9B6, Canada. Telephone: 905 430 5000. Fax: 905 430 5020.

Long renowned as the authoritative source for self-guided learning – with more than 30 million copies sold worldwide – the *Teach Yourself* series includes over 300 titles in the fields of languages, crafts, hobbies, business, computing and education.

British Library Cataloguing in Publication Data: a catalogue record for this title is available from the British Library.

Library of Congress Catalog Card Number: on file.

First published in UK 2004 by Hodder Headline Ltd, 338 Euston Road, London, NW1 3BH.

First published in US 2004 by Contemporary Books, a Division of the McGraw-Hill Companies, 1 Prudential Plaza, 130 East Randolph Street, Chicago, IL 60601 USA.

This edition published 2004.

The 'Teach Yourself' name is a registered trade mark of Hodder & Stoughton Ltd.

Typeset by Dorchester Typesetting Group Ltd.
Printed in Great Britain for Hodder & Stoughton Ltd, a division of Hodder Headline Ltd, 338 Euston Road, London NW1 3BH, by J. W. Arrowsmiths, Bristol.

Papers used in this book are natural, renewable and recyclable products. They are made from wood grown in sustainable forests. The logging and manufacturing processes conform to the environmental regulations of the country of origin.

Impression number   10 9 8 7 6 5 4 3 2 1

Year   2009 2008 2007 2006 2005 2004

contents

introduction

▶ The Classical, or Spanish, guitar is one of the loveliest instruments I know. Its attraction is hard to define; it is quiet, difficult to play and has rather an unbalanced repertoire due to its lapses from fashion in the eighteenth and nineteenth centuries. Perhaps part of its appeal is due to its being a totally unmechanical instrument in a mechanised and technological age: no bow, no pedals, no artificial aids at all – just played with flesh and nail. It is also extremely flexible, as it is not only portable, but needs no accompaniment. But for me, its greatest charm lies in its intimacy and its delicate nuance of tone. Andres Segovia himself said: 'It speaks to the heart with quiet simplicity.'

The guitar is such a familiar sound to us now that it is hard to believe that in the middle of the twentieth century, few music lovers considered it as a serious instrument. However, with the advent of pop music, a whole new world of sounds and cultures opened up, or in the case of the classical guitar, began to be rediscovered. Whereas the electric guitar was essentially a new, young, rather brash sound, exemplified in the music of Elvis Presley, there was also the earthy Blues guitar of artists such as Muddy Waters as well as the thrilling Flamenco music which also increased in popularity. At the same time, Folk music gained in public acceptance, with the sixties protest singers such as Bob Dylan and Joan Baez never seen without the indispensable guitar. Django Reinhardt, the virtuoso jazz guitarist provided another approach.

Perhaps it was this new recognition of the versatility of the guitar that triggered off the revival of interest in the classical guitar. The British guitarists, John Williams and Julian Bream, soon became known internationally. But the person who did more than anyone to rescue the guitar from oblivion was the great Spanish guitarist, Andres Segovia, through his legendary concerts and encouragement to contemporary composers to write for the instrument. Now, in the twenty-first century, the Spanish guitar again has the respect it deserves.

This book is designed for the complete beginner who should, by using it and the accompanying CD as a guide, and with regular practice, be able to enjoy playing this beautiful instrument at a standard of at least reasonable proficiency. I hope that the more ambitious student might also be encouraged to find a good teacher.

Although this book is written primarily for the classical guitarist, the technique described provides a foundation which can be easily adapted for guitarists with different interests.

the classical guitar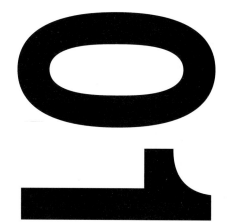

In this chapter you will learn about:

- parts of the guitar

- points to look for when choosing a guitar

- any extras you might need.

Parts of the guitar

Unlike other stringed instruments, it is essential that you buy a full-sized guitar, even for a ten-year-old. Small growing hands are, in any case, more adaptable than full-grown adult ones and they soon learn to stretch. In this way the distances between the frets are learnt and felt from the start, and also a far richer and more satisfying tone will be obtained from the larger instrument.

The full-sized guitar is about 25 inches from the nut to the bridge (see Figure 1) and the body of the instrument is at least 3½ inches deep from front to back at the widest point to give a strong tone. The fingerboard should be wide – about 2 inches – to allow plenty of room for the fingers to move about easily and to avoid touching more than one string at once.

The wood the guitar is made of is important, as it affects the quality and strength of the tone more than anything else. The front of the guitar, the soundboard, is made of fine-grained pine or spruce and varnished. The back and sides are of a more grainy wood; in the best guitars this is rosewood or walnut, in the cheaper ones mahogany, pine or layers of plywood. The neck is of a stronger wood, usually mahogany, the fingerboard of ebony. These strong woods serve a threefold purpose: to stop the neck from warping and causing buzzing; to prevent grooves from being worn into the fingerboard by constant finger pressure; and finally the black of the ebony helps to show up the strings. In cheaper guitars mahogany which has been dyed black is substituted for the ebony.

Points to look for when choosing a guitar

1 Check the size; in particular ensure that the fingerboard is wide enough and that the body is full-sized. Check the quality of the wood (this will be determined to some extent by the amount you are prepared to pay).

2 Listen to the tone. This is very important, and you might have to enlist the aid of the assistant here. Play each string individually and make sure that there are no buzzes. The tone should be strong, clear, vibrant and balanced; the low notes and the high notes should sound equally strongly. The bass (low) notes carry more in any case, and you must make sure that these are not so strong that they drown the treble (high) notes.

3 Hold the guitar horizontally – rather as if you were holding a violin – and squint up the instrument from bottom to top, making sure that it is straight from end to end. This ensures that there is no warping in the neck which causes, at the very least, a buzzing sound when you play.

4 Look at the back of the guitar; those of the better guitars are divided into two pieces in order to obtain a symmetrical grain either side of the middle line. This ensures a balanced tone. If the back is in one piece, choose a guitar with an even grain.

5 Test the 'action'. This means the distance you actually press the string down onto the fingerboard. You must do this yourself to feel it. Press each string down with the fingers of the left hand. It will probably be easy by the nut, but is it easy on the twelfth fret, the fret where the neck joins the body of the guitar? The action is very important; it can make a guitar easy or difficult to play.

6 Make sure that the back of the fingerboard is flattened, in order to accommodate the thumb easily.

7 Look at the bridge. See that it is strongly glued onto the front of the guitar. Look at the machine heads and try turning them. Do they adjust easily, not too stiffly and not so quickly that it takes ages to wind up a string? Look at the frets. Run a finger along the edge of the fingerboard and check that there are no rough bits. Do the same round the sound hole.

Remember that every guitar is different, even those of identical make, number and price.

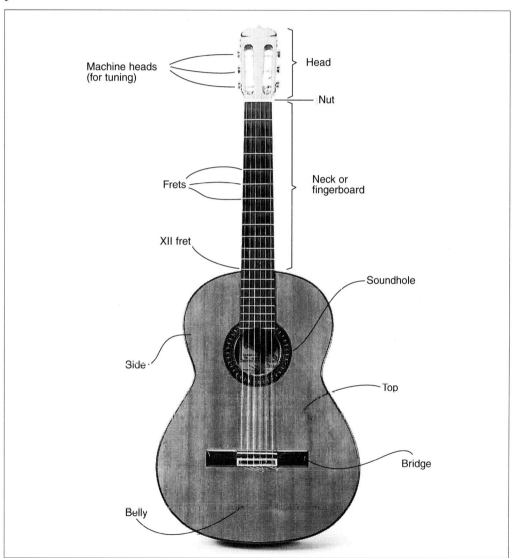

figure 1

Buying a guitar

Although it is possible to buy a reasonable guitar either second-hand or in general music shops, it is far more sensible to go to a specialist stockist where there is a much larger selection of instruments and where you will be able to get advice on the various makes available. Guitars are relatively cheap instruments, a fraction of the price of a piano or a wind instrument for example, and in the lower price range it is possible to buy a perfectly adequate instrument for a beginner. Obviously, the more you pay the more responsive and more resonant a guitar you will get. Unlike most instruments, high quality guitars do not increase in value with age; they do eventually wear out and have to be replaced and for this reason a second-hand instrument is not always a good investment. There are now many good, cheap Japanese guitars which are excellent value and these cheaper instruments seem to be more reliable than the Spanish ones of equivalent price. However, if you want a concert guitar, the Spanish makes of Ramirez, Fleta and Bellido are surely unequalled.

Miscellaneous extras

There are several other items that you will need, some of which you will have to buy and some of which you can improvise.

Guitar cases

There are two sorts, hard and soft. The soft ones are now normally made of plastic and are cheap to buy. Although waterproof, they offer little or no protection against knocks. If you can afford it, I do recommend a good hard case. They are expensive, but they do offer complete protection and last well. They have a padded lining and a small compartment for strings, etc. Although pretty well waterproof, I do slip mine into a large polythene bag during a real downpour. Do not be tempted by the cheap cardboard makes. They are just not worth the money, and I have seen them disintegrate in a few months.

Care of the guitar

Keep your guitar in its case. Never leave the guitar near a radiator or in the sun. Do not leave a chamois cloth in the case which will absorb the humidity. Do not keep the guitar in a damp or very cold place like a cellar or attic.

Strings

I sometimes think it would be a good thing if guitarists spent as much time playing their guitars as they do arguing about the merits of various strings and the length of their fingernails! The Spanish guitar is strung with a mixture of strings: the three bass strings are made of nylon covered with a tightly wound metal, the three treble strings of nylon only. It is possible to get the bass strings either polished or unpolished, the advantage of the polished ones being that they do not squeak when the fingers are slid up and down them. Those in favour of unpolished strings say that they have a more brilliant tone and last longer. Personally, I favour the polished strings, finding the squeaking both ugly and distracting. However, I know that male guitarists often prefer unpolished strings as their hands tend to sweat, thus 'darkening' the tone. Their hands are usually stronger than a woman's and the stronger pressure helps to lose the squeak. *Chacun à son goût.*

You will probably find that the strings on your new guitar are of poor quality and will need replacing almost immediately. Some players have very successful results in using combinations of strings – bass of one make and treble of another – finding through experience what suits their guitar best. Most shops selling good guitars have a wide selection of strings and will be pleased to advise you about them.

Footstools, music stands, tuning forks, metronomes and electronic guitar tuners

You will also need a footstool and a music stand. There are collapsible models of both available, which are very useful as they can be carried around easily. Alternatively, they could easily be improvised. A tuning fork in A is essential and quite cheap. I have found a tuning fork more satisfactory than pitch-pipes, which tend to go out of tune. A recent development is electronic guitar tuners which react to the sound waves when a string is played and either show a light or have a needle which indicates when the string is in tune. They are very straightforward to use and can be very helpful. Finally, you need a metronome. These are those strange machines that tick loudly to keep you in time with the music. However, they are expensive and might well be an item to save up for and buy later on.

Do remember to insure your new guitar; it will only cost a small amount a year and is well worth it.

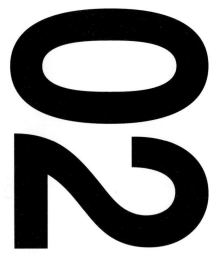

starting off

In this chapter you will learn:

- the names of the strings

- how to tune the guitar

- how to replace a string.

Some of the most basic points, such as tuning the newly acquired guitar, are so obvious that they sometimes tend to be taken for granted, which can lead to considerable frustration when you find that you can play a Bach fugue but cannot replace a string in order to do so!

► Naming the strings and tuning the guitar

There is quite an art to tuning an instrument accurately, and it will probably take some time for your ear to hear and analyse which string is out of tune. By pressing the string onto the fingerboard with the left-hand fingers, the length of the string is shortened and the pitch of the note thus raised. The right hand vibrates and sounds the strings. When the strings are played without using the left hand they are called *open strings*. The names of the open strings are: EADGBE, with an interval of two octaves between the two Es:

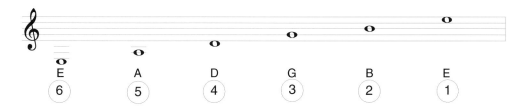

The strings are also identified by numbers in a circle.

There are several ways of tuning; one is to take the notes from the piano:

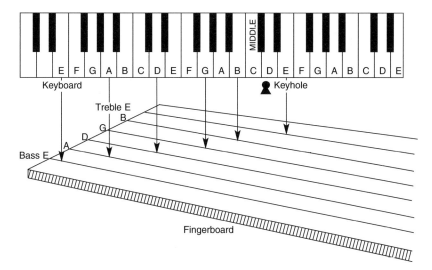

Remember that guitar music is written an octave higher than it sounds, and the equivalent notes on the piano (illustrated above) will be written thus:

Play the notes on the piano, starting from the bass E, and try to match the appropriate strings to the notes on the piano, one at a time. Sound the guitar string with your right hand, and if it sounds too high (i.e. sharp) loosen the string with your left hand by turning the tuning peg towards you; if it sounds too low (i.e. flat) tighten it by turning the tuning peg away from you. Adjust the string very gently; if you are loosening it, it is best to drop below the note you are aiming at first and then tighten the string again to the required note, otherwise the string tends to slip out of tune very quickly.

The main problem with taking the notes from the piano is that it is difficult to match up two different kinds of sound. The same problem arises with pitch-pipes. These are a set of very small pipes which sound the notes of the strings, but pitched an octave higher, when you blow them.

Another, and probably more accurate, way is to use a tuning fork for the A string and then tune the other strings by ear.

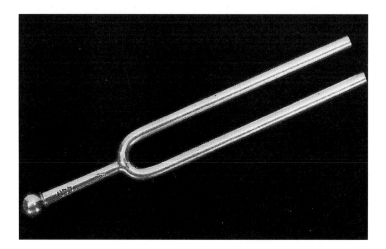

figure 2

To sound the tuning fork, hold the end firmly between the forefinger and thumb, being careful not to touch the forked part or it will not sound. Strike the forked end lightly on your knee, and then press the end of the fork on to a firm surface such as a table top and the note A will sound, one octave higher than open A. Try to match the A string to this sound as closely as you can.

To tune the D string, stop the A string on the fifth fret, which is the note D. Now play the open D string, and if the two notes do not sound the same adjust the open string until they do.

To tune the G string, use the same method but, instead, stop the D string on the fifth fret.

To find the B, stop the G string on the *fourth* fret and then match the sounds. The difference in the frets is due to the difference in intervals between the strings; the interval between G and B is a third (GAB), whereas the interval between the other strings is in each case a fourth.

To find the top E, stop the B string on the fifth fret and tune the open string. Bottom E should sound like top E, only two octaves lower.

Remember to tune the open string, not the string you are stopping. Sometimes it helps to hum or whistle the steps up between the open strings, even if you cannot sing well, as it will help you to hear the distance between the strings.

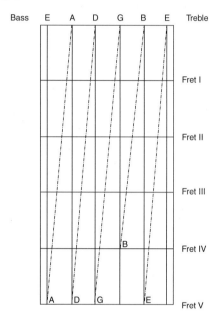

Stop the strings at the points marked to
make the sound of the next open string

Memory aid

All this sounds rather complicated, but in practice it is quite straightforward. Remember that the principle is to use the string that is already in tune to help you tune the next one. Your ear will soon learn the sounds you are trying to get and you will be able to tune up very quickly. However, never rush yourself; nothing sounds worse than an out-of-tune guitar.

How to replace a string

When replacing a set of strings, remove and change one string at a time, so as not to cause too much strain on the bridge. You will see that the covered strings have a soft uncovered part at one or both ends. Use this uncovered end to thread through the little hole in the bridge. Twist the uncovered piece of string over the covered part a couple of times, thus securing the string at the bridge. Try to imitate the way in which the strings are already attached. Take the string over the bridge, through the grooves at the bridge and nut, and thread it through the hole in the appropriate tuning peg, pulling it taut. With the nylon strings it is wise to tie them once, as they tend to slip otherwise. Hold the spare end of the string firmly behind the guitar and wind the peg in an anticlockwise direction until the string is taut and the spare end of string is caught. The best time to change strings is in the evening, leaving them taut but untuned overnight and then tuning them very gently the following day. In this way the covered strings expand evenly and do not expose the nylon thread inside, which is what happens if they are tuned too quickly. The strings take some time to stretch and you will need to tune as often as possible for a couple of days.

A string does not necessarily have to be broken to need replacing; after a certain amount of use, the tone goes dead and does not 'sing' any more. Change the strings when they are dirty or worn. As far as breakages go, you will find that the D string breaks far more frequently than the others; apart from being the longest covered string and therefore subject to the most tension, it is also played the most. If you are playing your guitar every day, you will probably need a complete set of strings every 6 weeks and several extra D strings. If your hands sweat a lot, the strings will wear out and break more quickly.

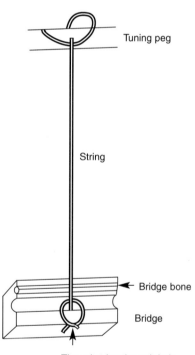

Tuning peg

String

Bridge bone

Bridge

Thread string through hole

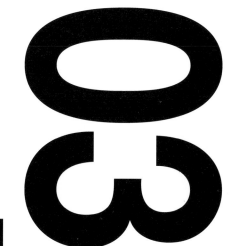

textures in sound

In this chapter you will learn:

• the meaning of scales, chords and arpeggios.

▶ Scales, chords and arpeggios

It is possible to make many different textures of sound in music: single-note passages, notes in groups or notes in clumps played simultaneously. These different textures are formed basically by the *scale*, the *chord* or the *arpeggio*.

The scale

As you know, a scale is a chain of notes ascending or descending in steps. A scale can start from any of the twelve notes you have found on the stopped strings; the first note of the scale is called the *key note* and gives its name to the scale for instance, the scale of C.

There are two types of scale, each with its own particular sound formed by its own particular pattern of semitones and tones. They are called major (sounding rather cheerful) and minor (sounding rather melancholy). As the intervals between the notes are unequal, sharps or flats have to be added in certain places to make the semitones come at the same point in each scale. These sharps or flats are grouped together at the beginning of the scale and are called the key signature. Thus a scale starting on C is said to be in the *key* of C major or C minor, depending on the key signature. The key of a piece of music is decided in a similar way, although a piece usually ends, rather than begins, on the key note.

The construction of scales and their key signatures is discussed at greater length in Chapter 16.

Chords

A chord is the simultaneous combination of two or more notes. They are written one above another like this:

Broken chords

A broken chord is a chord where the notes are played separately but not in the order in which they appear in a scale:

Arpeggios

An arpeggio is a chord where the notes are played separately, in order, like on a harp.

As scales, chords and arpeggios form such a vital part in the structure of a piece of music, it is important to make them part of everyday practice. However, a scale or arpeggio would not necessarily appear in full in a piece of music but more often in a fragmented form.

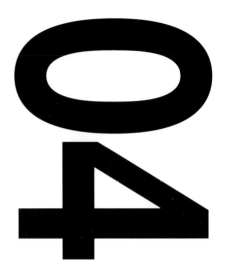

the right hand

> In this chapter you will learn:
>
> • the importance of fingernails
>
> • how the fingers are numbered
>
> • the two basic movements: apoyando and tirando.

Fingernails

One of the most valuable natural assets that a guitarist can have is good strong fingernails. There is great controversy amongst guitarists over their precise length and strength or hardness, but they are undoubtedly essential to a good tone. The reason is that the right hand vibrates and sounds the strings, using a combination of flesh (the finger tip) and nail. Some schools of thought maintain that the nails should be so long and hard that they alone should touch the string. However, to my ear this nearly always produces a very hard and often weak tone, rather as if the string has been vibrated by a plectrum. The undoubted advantage of very long nails is that you can play very fast very easily, more or less scratching over the strings. Personally, I prefer the richer and more carrying tone produced by the flesh-plus-nail combination.

Apart from the actual length of the nails, more than one school of thought exists as to how hard they should be. Segovia himself said they should be soft but strong, not breaking easily. However, other, albeit less revered, sources suggest they should be as hard as possible, arguing that the soft nail bends on the string, thus producing a twangy tone. The arguments are endless, but nails of some sort must be grown.

Bad nails can be much improved by keeping them out of hot water and by protecting them whenever possible with gloves. There are many chemical products on the market for strengthening nails and the individual must find for himself what suits him best. A word of warning: some of the nail hardeners tend to make the nail not only very hard but also very brittle; creams that help to strengthen the growth of the nail seem to be more effective in the long run.

As a general rule, the right-hand nails should be just long enough to be seen above the finger tip when you hold your hand up, palm facing you, fingers straight (see Figure 3). The left-hand nails should be kept short enough for the fingers to press the strings down onto the fingerboard easily.

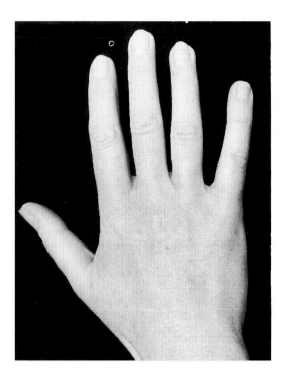

figure 3

Keep the right-hand nails filed in an oval shape, all the same length. A fine emery board is far less abrasive than a metal nail-file.

I once had a young male pupil who was going to give a concert and broke all his fingernails in a train door the morning before he was due to perform. Being an enterprising young man, he hurried to the nearest beauty salon, where he demanded a set of false nails! They were duly applied and the concert went smoothly, but unfortunately the nails set like rock and he could not get them off for a month. This remedy is only recommended for dire emergencies!

The two basic movements – apoyando and tirando

There are two basic ways of vibrating the strings with the right hand. They are called *apoyando*, meaning striking, when the fingers are kept fairly straight, and *tirando*, meaning plucking, when you play with bent fingers. In general, apoyando is used for scale and single-note passages, and tirando for chordal and arpeggio passages. However, it does depend on the context, and no hard and fast rule can be laid down. The hand must be positioned in such a way as to be able to move from one of these movements to the other without difficulty; and also in such a way that the three fingers and thumb can move freely, making even contact with the strings. Remember that the third finger (in both hands) is by far the weakest.

How the fingers are numbered

The fingers of the right hand are most frequently indicated by the initial of the Spanish words for the fingers:

Thumb	*pulgar*	*p*
Index finger	*indice*	*i*
Middle finger	*medio*	*m*
Third/ring finger	*anular*	*a*

Other signs often used in printed music are:

p	V	+ or □	thumb
i	I	.	first finger
m	I I	. .	second finger
a	I.I	. . .	third finger

The little finger is rarely used.

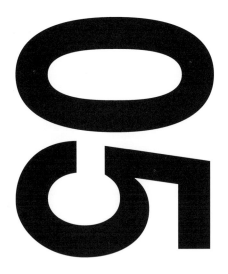

apoyando

In this chapter you will learn:

- how to hold the guitar

- the position of the right hand

- the names of the open strings

- simple exercises for the right hand alone.

▶ The position of the right hand and simple exercises

1 Rest the elbow comfortably on the side of the guitar, letting the hand fall over the sound hole. Straighten the fingers and thumb so that the hand lies flat on the strings (see Figure 4).

2 Turn the hand, *from the wrist*, until the fingers are pointing straight down and are at right angles to the strings and parallel to the frets, keeping the thumb pointing towards the head of the guitar (see Figure 5).

3 Stand the fingers on their tips, keeping the thumb forward. The fingers should be kept straight. Keep the wrist arched and the hand relaxed. You must be able to move your fingers quickly from the lowest to the highest strings without adjusting your hand position, and the height of your wrist determines this. Experiment to find what feels most comfortable. Remember to keep your fingers parallel to the frets (see Figure 6).

figure 4

figure 5

figure 6

4 Move your fingers back until they rest on the A string. Using finger *i*, press the A string back until your finger rests on the string behind (the E string) and the A string is released (see Figure 7). Now press the A string down with *m*, then

figure 7

Memory aid

figure 8

again with *i* (see Figure 8). Do not press too hard because you will get an ugly twanging effect. Swing the fingers up high in front as they swap over, so as not to touch the vibrating string and cause a buzzing sound.

figure 9

5 When this movement becomes easy, try to change strings. Move to the D string simply as if you were walking up a step, alternating your fingers. When you can strike this string successfully, move on to the other three treble strings. Make sure that your wrist remains high enough for your fingers to change strings without your hand having to move. Keep your thumb forward: this keeps it out of the way and keeps your hand round (see Figure 9).

6 If your hand feels tired or stiff, rest it for a few minutes; it cannot function properly if it is at all tense.

Now try striking each string five times, starting with the A string, playing up to top E and back down again. Make sure that you alternate your fingers when you change to a lower string in the same way as you do when moving to a higher string; this will ensure that the spaces between the notes are even and that the tone is clear.

Listen carefully to the sounds you are making; the tone should be strong and clear and even in tone and tempo, not three soft, short notes and two long, loud ones. Make sure that you do not touch the vibrating string with your non-playing fingers.

7 When you have mastered apoyando with *im*, try with *ma*, alternating in the same way; it is important to strengthen the third finger.

tirando

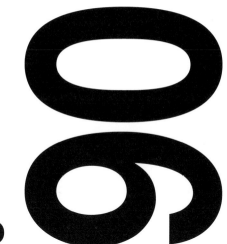

In this chapter you will learn:

• how to play arpeggios, broken chords and chords.

▶ How to play arpeggios, broken chords and chords

The word tirando actually means 'pulling, stretching, drawing back'. Guitarists often describe it as 'plucking', but this is not really entirely accurate as it tends to suggest a pulling away movement; it is rather more an upward hooking movement. The best guide, as always, is your ear; the tone should be round and full, not twanging and harsh. One of the commonest faults for the beginner is to put his fingers into the strings too far, thus forcing him to tear at the strings in order to get any sound at all. However, with practice, the fingers soon find their own depth.

Memory aid

figure 10a

1 Use the same position as for apoyando, but bend your fingers and place the finger tips *ima* on the treble strings GBE and the thumb on bass string E (see Figures 10a and 10b).

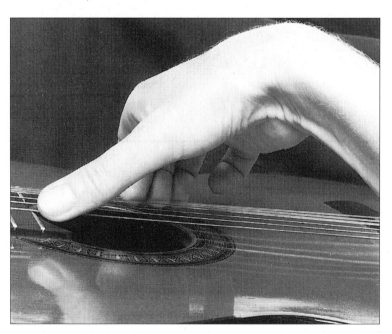

figure 10b

Memory aid

figure 11

2 Keeping the thumb firm, but not bent, swing it upwards, sounding the bass E as you do so with the side of the thumb (see Figure 11). Then sound *ima* consecutively, by drawing them upwards, sounding the strings with the finger tips and in such a way as to avoid touching the other strings. A common fault at first is to play *a* by jerking the hand, thus making an ugly sound and also forcing you to adjust position in order to recommence playing. The hand should remain quite still and relaxed while the fingers do the work. Finger *a* will eventually get stronger.

3 Replace *pima* simultaneously. Do not put in the thumb first and then the fingers; this nearly always causes the beginner to turn his hand round so as to be parallel to the strings instead of the frets, thus making it difficult for him to have an even contact with the strings. When you have replaced your fingers

figure 12a

satisfactorily, repeat the movement *pima* over and over again until it feels easy and sounds smooth and even. This will take some time, so do not hesitate to rest when you feel at all tired. You will find a mirror very useful at this stage, as not only will you be able to check that your hand is in the correct position but also you will learn to play by feel rather than by watching your hand. This

figure 12b

figure 12c

is absolutely essential, and the habit cannot be formed too soon. If you seem to be playing the wrong strings, make sure that there are no gaps between your fingers; as soon as they start spacing themselves out, you will be unable to feel the distance between the strings. Try to make the gaps between the notes the same length as the notes themselves; play very slowly so that you can replace your fingers and continue playing without any noticeable break in the sound (see Figures 12a, 12b and 12c).

The notes you are playing look like this on the manuscript:

Exercise 1

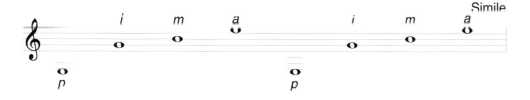

Simile = repeat this phrase

Now you want to try new finger combinations. The reverse movements of the previous one is *pami*:

Exercise 2

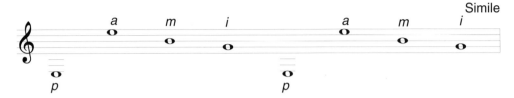

In each case, practise the movement until it feels, and sounds, easy before moving on to a new one. Be especially careful not to have a long pause between each sequence whilst you reinsert your fingers.

The combination of the first two movements looks like this:

Exercise 3

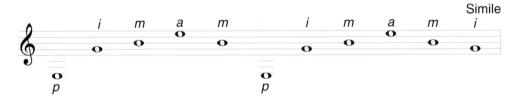

The way to get the smoothest connection between the two movements is to use finger *a* as a pivot. Put in *pima* as before, play *pim*, but *before* playing finger *a* reinsert *i* and *m*. Then play *ami*. Thus:

Exercise 4

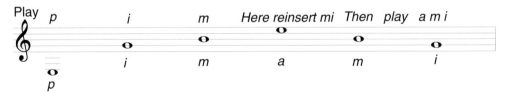

This method has the twofold advantage of making the join smoother than if you merely played all the fingers up and then played *mi* individually, and of making it much easier for your fingers to find the correct strings when you are playing quickly. You will probably notice how the sound is much more connected when you put your fingers in the strings together before playing them than when you play the strings individually. Obviously there are occasions when you want the sound to be more disconnected, but arpeggios are normally played smoothly unless marked otherwise.

Another useful movement, which helps you to learn how to place your fingers quickly, is:

Exercise 5

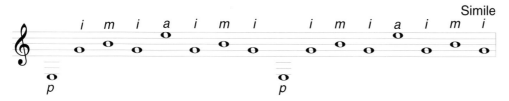

Here, the fingers are inserted in pairs, the middle pair stretching to the top string.

You will find it far more profitable to practise and perfect one movement at a time than to dodge from one to another. Practise slowly and listen carefully.

When you play a chord, in other words when you play the notes simultaneously, the notes are written on top of each other like this:

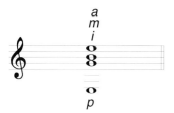

Try to play the following exercises. Remember to keep the thumb straight, swinging it upwards.

Exercise 6

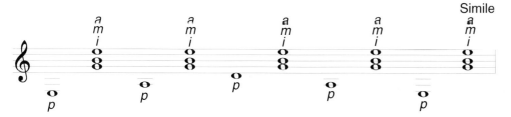

At first, you might tend to tear at the chord; this is often because your fingers are too straight. Remember to bend your fingers and to keep your wrist high and arched. Do not move your hand; keep it still and relaxed whilst your fingers do the work.

Try this movement when you have mastered the last one:

Exercise 7

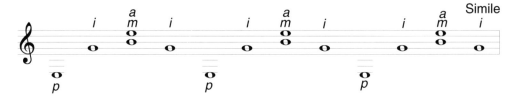

Finally, when all these movements feel easy and sound good, try combining apoyando and tirando:

Exercise 8

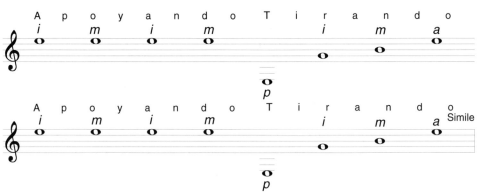

I have started apoyando with *i* so that the other fingers fall on the appropriate strings for the arpeggio.

Try to perfect all these movements *before* adding any simple chords in the left hand.

Playing five- and six-string chords

There are two alternatives when playing chords with more than five notes: either the thumb can stroke across all the strings, or the thumb can play two or three bass notes followed by the fingers playing the remaining notes. If the second method is used, it is easier for the thumb to press down into each successive string in order to connect the sound. Care must be taken to ensure that every note sounds equally. Personally, I find the second method best for chords needing a rich, full tone and the first method best for fast, 'sudden' chords.

Frequently, chords have to be played on strings that are not adjacent, so that the fingers have to spread out (see Figure 13).

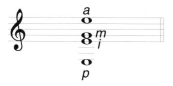

figure 13

The right hand techniques is by far the most controversial aspect of playing the guitar. The position that I have described seems to me the most logical, since in this way the strings are vibrated in the same way as a bow vibrates any other stringed instrument – at right angles across the strings. It also facilitates the fingers to make any combination of movements with equal ease and speed. However, other teachers will teach other positions; more than one road leads to Rome. As always, you must be guided by your tone. But do not adjust the position of your hand until you have been playing for at least a year; initially, the position will feel strange through sheer unfamiliarity.

Suggested easy studies for the right hand

Tirando

Sor, *20 Studies*, edited by Segovia: No. IV (Augener-Galliard).
Giuliani, *24 Studies, Opus 48*: Nos. 5 & 12 (Schotts GA, 32).
Carcassi, *25 Melodious and Progressive Studies, Opus 60*: No. 3 (Schotts GA, 2).
Carcassi, *6 Caprices, Opus 26* (Schotts GA, 72).
Pujol, *El Abejorro* (Ricordi)   ⎫ more
Villa-Lobos, *Douze Études*: No. 1 (Max Eschig) ⎬ advanced.

Apoyando

Carcassi, *25 Melodious and Progressive Studies, Opus 60*: No. 1 (Schotts GA, 2).
Tarrega, *Estudio de Velocidad* (Biblioteca Fortea).

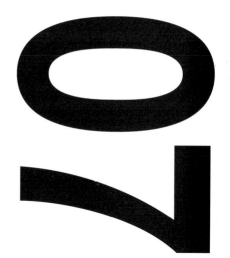

simple theory

In this chapter you will learn:

* how to read notes on the manuscript.

Note reading

There are two main stages in reading music: the first is to actually decipher the dot on the page, its name and length; the second is to find the note on the guitar and play it. At first it seems to take ages and can become rather disheartening, but with practice your coordination becomes quicker and quicker until it is a reflex action. You will not need to play from music immediately in any case, as you will be concentrating mainly on your right hand and just using very simple chord shapes in your left hand (see Chapters 04 and 05). Do not confuse yourself by trying to learn too many notes at once. Learn two or three notes on the music, then try to play them. In this way you will soon grasp the relationship between the notes and progress quickly.

The notes in music are named after the first seven letters of the alphabet: ABCDEFG, rising stepwise in ascending order from A to G. After G the note pattern repeats from A, making the same sounds but eight notes higher. This distance of eight notes from a note to its twin eight notes higher (or lower) is called an octave. An octave can be from any note, not just from A (see diagram on page 32). The two outside strings on the guitar are tuned two octaves apart, and the guitar has an overall compass of three and a half octaves from its lowest to its highest note. The chain of notes joining a note to its twin an octave higher is called a *scale*, from the Latin word *scala* meaning 'ladder'.

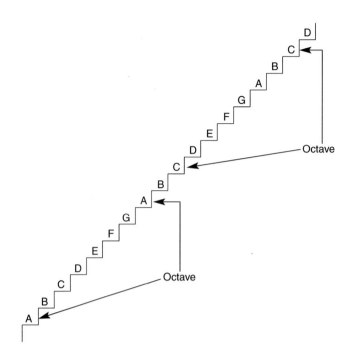

Music is written on special paper called *manuscript* paper, which looks like this:

As you can see, the lines are in groups of five separated by four spaces. These five lines and four spaces are known collectively as the *stave* or *staff* and provide the framework on which music is written. The notes are placed either astride the lines or in the spaces; the actual pitch of the notes – that is to say, how high or low they are in relation to one another – is determined by a sign at the beginning of each line called a *clef*, from the French word meaning 'key'.

The two clefs most commonly used are the *treble clef*, which is used for the higher registers such as a woman's voice or for the right hand if you are playing the piano, and the *bass clef*, which is used for the lower registers such as a man's voice or for the left hand on the piano. Guitar music is written entirely in the treble clef, although the notes are sounded an octave lower than they are actually written. Sometimes there is a little number 8 under the treble clef to indicate this:

There is now a note on every line and space. The lowest line on the stave is E. The notes ascend one step at a time, and correspondingly one letter of the alphabet at a time; to the top line F. (Do not forget that after G the note pattern starts from A again.) Any notes higher than top F or lower than bottom E are written on additional lines called *leger lines*. Just continue to name the lines and spaces after the letters of the alphabet.

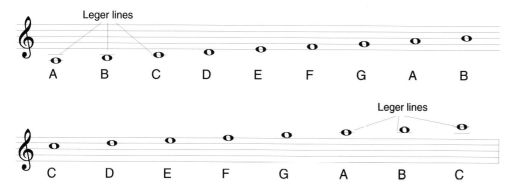

Many people find it easier to learn the lines and spaces separately:

Lines:

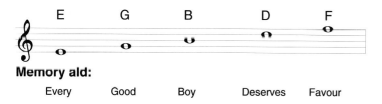

Memory aid:

Every   Good   Boy   Deserves   Favour

Spaces:

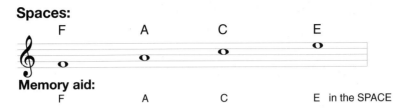

Memory aid:

F   A   C   E in the SPACE

Tone and semitones

The distance or step between any two notes is called an *interval*. The intervals between the neighbouring pairs of notes are not all equal and are described either as a *tone* or as a *semitone*. A semitone is the smallest distance commonly used in Western music; the interval of a tone is equal in pitch to two semitones.

On the guitar the interval of a semitone is marked by a fret, so that the interval of a tone means that you move your finger two frets.

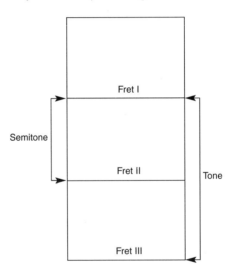

The following example shows where the interval between two notes is a tone and where it is only a semitone:

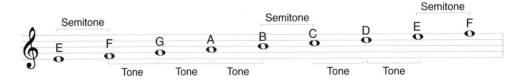

Memory aid: The semitones fall between E and F, and between B and C

Accidentals – sharps, flats and naturals

An accidental is a sign placed immediately before a note indicating a temporary change in its pitch. The sharps and flats on the piano are represented by the black notes; on the guitar you merely alter the note by moving your finger one fret up or down. The note itself retains its name, adding the word sharp, flat or natural as is appropriate, for example, F sharp.

Sharps

A sharp (♯) raises a note a semitone. For instance, G becomes G sharp. To play G sharp on the guitar you must move your finger up one fret towards the guitar body.

A double sharp (𝄪) raises a note two semitones (one tone). See also Chapter 16.

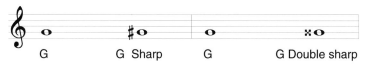

G   G Sharp   G   G Double sharp

Flats

A flat (♭) lowers a note a semitone. For instance, G becomes G flat. To play G flat on the guitar you move your finger one fret down towards the tuning pegs from G.

A double flat (♭♭) lowers a note two semitones (one tone). See also Chapter 16.

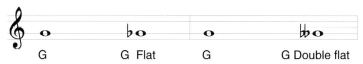

G   G Flat   G   G Double flat

Naturals

A natural (♮) restores a note to its natural pitch if it has been raised or lowered previously:

G Sharp   G Natural

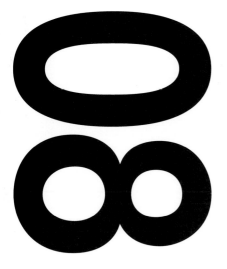

fretwork

In this chapter you will learn:

- how to find the notes on the guitar.

How to find the notes on the guitar

The first notes you must be able to recognise are the *open strings* – that is to say, the strings when sounded by the right hand without stopping them with the left hand. Learn the notes by sight and try to pick them out on the guitar with your right hand.

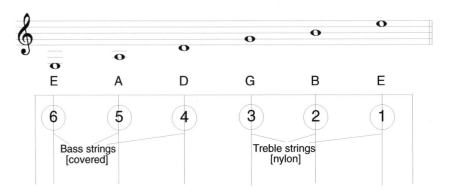

Strings are often referred to by the numbers shown, usually in a circle to differentiate them from fingerings

When you are able to identify the open strings immediately, you can begin to use the stopped strings. Start with the A string. Place your index finger on the first fret, the fret nearest the head of the guitar. You are now playing A sharp. Now slide your finger to the next fret, B. Similarly to the third fret, which is C. Remember that there is only a semitone between B and C, and between E and F.

Continue sliding your finger up one fret at a time as far as you can reach.

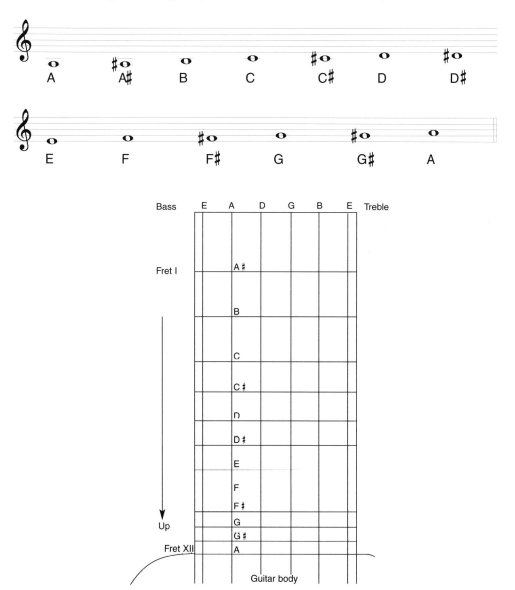

Now try the same thing on the B string. When you put your finger on the first fret, remember that you are now playing C.

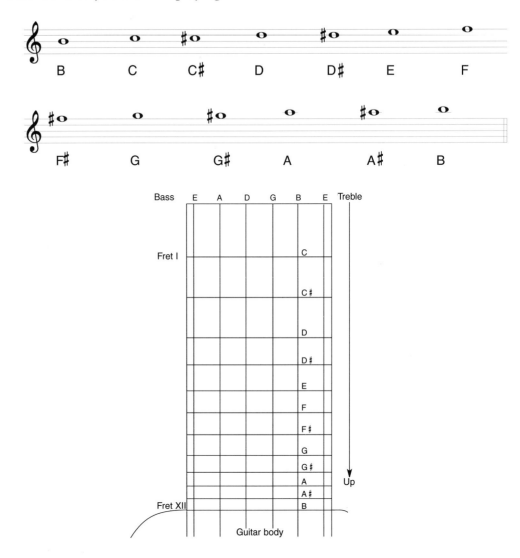

Try the same thing on each string.

Now try placing your finger on the twelfth fret, the fret nearest the body of the guitar; it is usually marked by a dot on the side of the guitar. Now slide your finger down – that is to say, back towards the head of the guitar – and name the notes in descending order. As you will lower each note by a semitone, you will call them by their flat names.

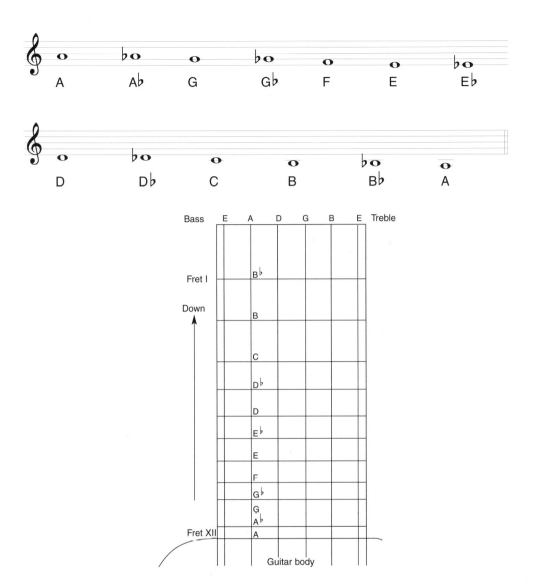

Again, experiment on each string in turn. Remember this is to help you understand the system of the notation rather than to teach you the names of every single note; this will only come slowly.

Enharmonic

This is a term used to describe the difference in the name of a note when its pitch stays the same. For instance, if you played the note on the first fret of the A string, you could call the note B flat or A sharp. The name of the note is determined by which key it is in.

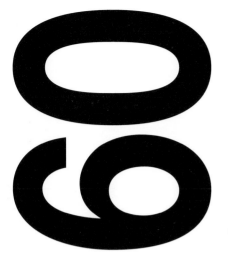

the left hand

In this chapter you will learn:

• the position of the left hand

• how the fingers are numbered.

Position of the left hand – how the fingers are numbered

The left hand has to be in such a position as to be able to move across the fingerboard and up and down the frets with agility and ease. The way to do this is to keep the hand more or less parallel to the fingerboard and the fingers parallel to the frets, so that the fingers can move in any direction quickly.

The fingers are numbered 1234 from the index finger. An open string is marked O.

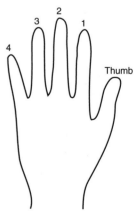

1 Place your fingers flat on the fingerboard near the first fret, keeping the fingers parallel to the frets. You will realise that you will have to turn the wrist slightly in order to do this.

The shoulder, arm and elbow should at all times hang naturally and be completely relaxed. A common fault is to lift the elbow when playing a difficult chord, which is, in fact, more a hindrance than a help. As with the right hand, the fingers do the work.

figure 14

2 The thumb supports the hand. With the ball of the thumb, feel the 'spine' of the fingerboard, which is in the middle of the back; usually the fingerboard is flatter there. The thumb should be opposite the first finger so that the other fingers can stretch away from it, and so that the thumb can help the first finger to press the strings in barrée playing (see Chapter 14). Do not let your thumb bend, or try to support it on the tip, as this is very tiring and totally ineffectual.

3 Now that you have the position of the hand you can see how to position your fingers. Stand each finger on its tip, bending the top joint so that the finger is at right angles to the fingerboard. You will now be able to feel if your nails are short enough. Place one finger on each fret, from the first fret to the fourth on the same string and as near to the frets as possible without actually pressing on them. If you press the strings a long way away from the frets they will buzz, while if you place your fingers on the frets themselves you will get a rather dead sound.

Your hand should now look like this:

figure 15

Notice in particular that the hand hangs straight down and the wrist is bent.

The hand should always be as close to the side of the fingerboard as possible without touching it, so that the fingers are right on their tips to get a clear, unmuffled tone and so that you can move quickly to another position. It is essential to be as accurate and precise as possible, otherwise you will never produce a clear tone or be able to play with any speed. It is most important to take these initial stages very slowly, since bad habits formed now are very difficult to break later on.

The spaces between each finger, and the muscles of the fingers themselves, will only improve and develop with steady and patient practice; the stretch between the third and fourth fingers in particular will need a great deal of work. Do not let your hand slip round like this:

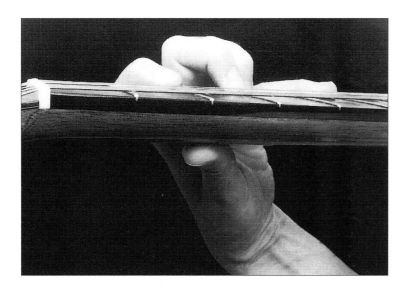

figure 16a

or this:

figure 16b

Although you might be able to get away with a few simple chords, your hand extension will never get any better.

hands together

In this chapter you will learn:

* how to play scales

* how to recognise common faults.

► How to play scales – finding the notes

The best way to start using your left hand is to play a scale. Regular scale practice is essential for speed and accuracy, quite apart from making your fingers supple.

The first scale to learn is C major, which has no sharps or flats. You will see on the music that the first octave looks like this:

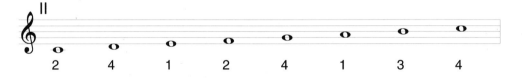

The Arabic numerals refer to the fingers; the Roman numeral II refers to the fret or position of the hand. This is slightly complicated as the fret referred to does not necessarily apply to the finger over which it is written but rather to the fret on which the *first* (*index*) finger rests. In this case it would look like this:

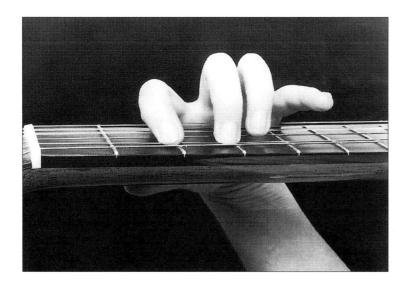

figure 17

If you think of one fret for one finger it is easy to understand.

One difficulty is to know which string to use. In this case, if your first finger is in the second position (II), your second finger, which plays the first note, middle C, will obviously fall onto the third fret, and so middle C must be somewhere on the third fret. If you count three semitones up the A string, you will find that middle C is on the third fret of that string.

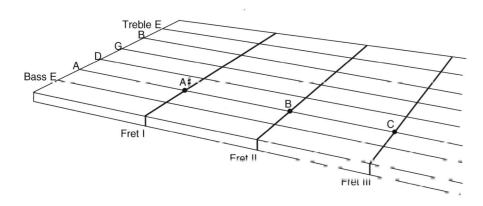

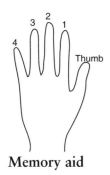

Memory aid

Once you have found middle C the rest is easy.

Scales are played apoyando, and I suggest that, to begin with, you strike each note three times, trying to make each note the same length and tone.

After playing middle C, use the fingers marked, remembering to miss out a fret if a finger is omitted. When you play the first finger, change to the next string.

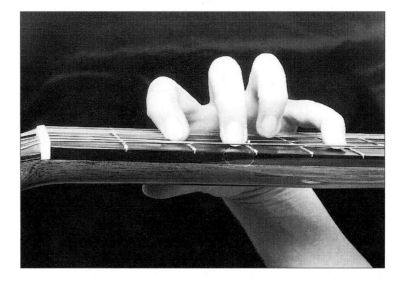

figure 18

Listen carefully to see that there are no buzzing notes; these are caused by inaccurate placing of the fingers or by not pressing hard enough.

Remember to keep your hand parallel to the fingerboard, and to keep it bent as near to the side of the fingerboard as possible. You will find this more difficult as your hand moves over to the higher strings, and you must try very hard to keep your fingers stretched out. You will also have to adjust your thumb as you move across the strings.

Do not release your fingers between the notes, keep them pressed down until you change strings; this helps to keep the strings in position. If the string is pulled out of its natural position, the sound is distorted.

To play the scale descending, simply release the higher notes in turn. When you can play one octave ascending and descending, and preferably by heart so that you can see what you are doing and correct any mistakes, you can try the rest of the scale – that is to say, two more octaves. You will see that, when a new fret is indicated, the fingers are joined by a short black line, like this:

This means that the first finger stays on the same string and slides (in this case) to the seventh fret. You will be able to hear that, although your hand has changed position completely by sliding from the second to the seventh fret, the sound has only moved up one more step, in other words one tone, from C to D.

As your finger slides, keep your hand parallel to the fingerboard and support it with your thumb, still keeping it opposite the first finger. The higher frets are narrower than the lower ones and you will have to contract your hand a little. Keep your fingers as bent as possible and your hand as near to the fingerboard as possible so that your fingers are right on their tips, holding the strings down firmly; the strings are liable to move unexpectedly at this point because you are such a long way from the nut which holds the strings tighter on the lower frets. When you play the very high notes above the twelfth fret, you will have to distort your hand a little in order to reach the notes (see Figure 19).

When playing the notes in descending order, release your fingers on the higher notes, as before, so that you can play the lower notes. When you reach your first finger, slide it back to the fret marked on the music and add any necessary fingers.

Sliding down is harder than sliding up, as the hand tends to swing back away from the fingerboard. Make sure that your fingers are suspended over the string on which you are sliding, otherwise you will have to reposition your hand completely for the next note (or chord). Slides have to be very fast, otherwise there is a gap in the music; you must know exactly which fret you are sliding to, and you must practise the slide by itself until it is absolutely accurate. When you are more experienced you will be able to feel the number of frets your fingers slide over, so that you can slide without looking at the frets. If the string squeaks when you slide, briefly release the pressure before sliding; remember that a slide should be smooth, silent and speedy.

figure 19

When you can play the scale of C easily you can move on to the others. Try only one at a time, and perfect it before you attempt a new one.

Common faults

Dead or muffled notes are often caused by placing the finger on the fret itself instead of next to it, by not pressing the string down hard enough or by touching the string with another finger.

Buzzing notes are often caused by placing the finger too far from the fret or by not bending the fingers enough, so that they are not at right angles to the fingerboard.

The top note is often dead or muffled either because it is being inadvertently touched by a finger or because it is not being stopped firmly enough.

When you are able to play the scales and broken chords with ease, it is time to attempt some easy pieces. A list of suggested music to choose from is given at the end of Chapter 12.

making music

In this chapter you will learn:

- how to play chords

- more advanced exercises using arpeggios and broken chords in the right hand

- how to read simple music.

▶ How to play chords – starting to read music

The following chords are easy ones to start with:

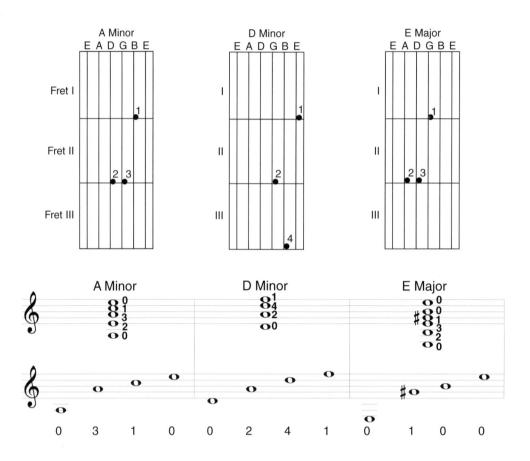

When you have learnt the positions of the left-hand fingers on the fingerboard, you can try using any of the right-hand broken chord and arpeggio movements that you learnt in Chapter 06, such as the following exercises. Remember that the left hand will keep still; it only moves when the chord changes, as indicated.

Exercise 9

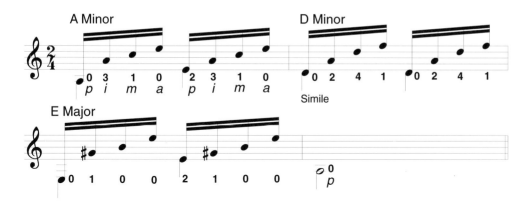

Exercise 10

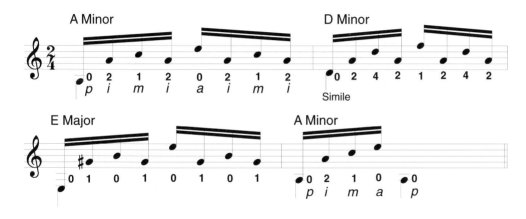

When you are able to play these chords easily, try stretching your hand by playing these chords of C and G major:

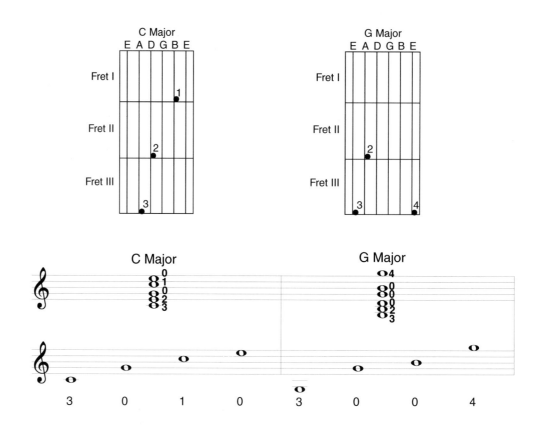

Practise changing from chord to chord quickly so that there is no break in the rhythm of the music.

In Exercise 11 the curved line and number 6 over the first two bars mean that you have to play six semiquavers to a beat instead of four semiquavers to a beat. Accent the first and third notes of each right-hand movement *pim*, *ami*. See also Chapter 13, 'Triplets'.

All the arpeggio movements illustrated so far are suitable for all types of guitar music although obviously those using a plectrum will have to adapt the right hand. Whichever type of guitar you are playing, first practise these chords until they are well established and then try using them to accompany a simple tune such as a

Exercise 11

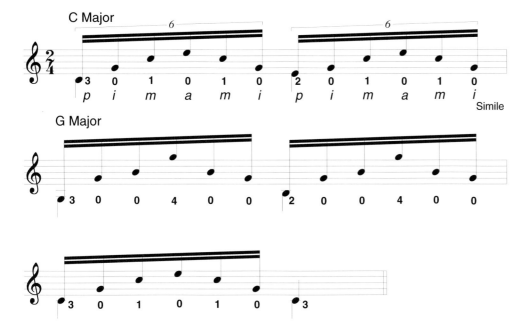

nursery rhyme or carol; the rhythm must be adapted as necessary. At first you will have to experiment to find the correct chord but soon you will find your ear becomes more selective. Gradually you will be able to enlarge your chord repertoire. It is advisable to buy a good chord book – you will find the type showing the chord written in manuscript as well as the chord position on the fingerboard the most useful.

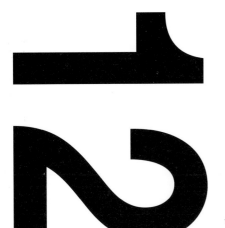

your first piece

In this chapter you will learn:

- how to play a simple piece

- how to finger it

- what you might find difficult.

▶ This piece, *Allegro*, by Giuliani, is an excellent piece to start with. It is dealt with fully on the CD.

The chords: A minor, D minor and E major are all familiar to you. The right hand is played tirando *pim ia im a*, which you learnt to play in Chapter 06. The chords and the right-hand movements are written on the manuscript.

First of all, look through to see which chords you know; I have marked them on the manuscript for you, but normally you will have to do this yourself. You will notice that the third finger is not used to form A minor in this case.

You also need to see whether the right hand plays tirando or apoyando and mark them too. I have ringed the fingers which you insert together.

I have also marked the places in bars 4 and 8 where there are small changes to the chords.

In the last line, you will see a straight line which connects the second finger from A to G sharp, indicating that you slide the finger between these two notes.

All printed music will have at least a minimum amount of fingering, but do not be afraid to question it, especially if you are aiming at a particular tone quality.

When you are satisfied that you understand what is going on in the manuscript, listen to the CD which gives detailed guidance on how to play *Allegro*.

When you can play *Allegro* try to finger *Arietta* on page 69. There are further ideas on how to finger more advanced pieces in Chapter 21.

Allegro

Giuliani

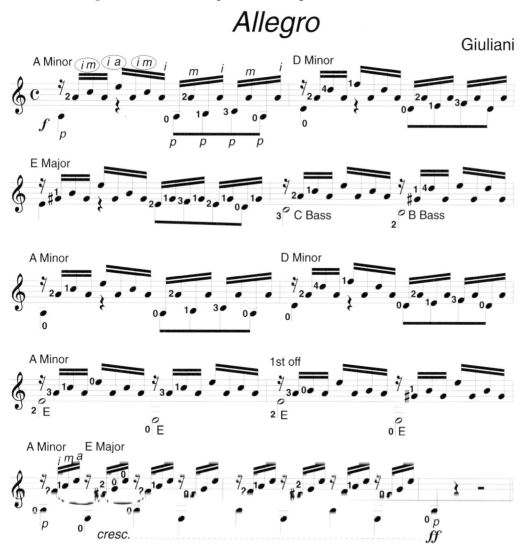

Albums of pieces by various composers

Otto Henrich Noetzal, *Meister des Gitarrenspiel I* (Verlag Wilhelmshaven) – 15 easy pieces.

Otto Henrich Noetzal, *Meister des Gitarrenspiel II* (Verlag Wilhelmshaven) – moderate difficulty.

The Guitarists Hour, Book I (Schotts GA, 19) – very easy.

The Guitarists Hour, Book II (Schotts GA, 20) – easy.

The Guitarists Hour, Book III (Schotts GA, 21) – medium.

World's Favourite Series for Classical Guitar (Ashley Publication No. 43) – wide range of difficulty.

Collections of pieces by individual composers

Carcassi, *12 Easy Pieces, Opus 10* (Schotts GA, 73).

Carcassi, *54 Selected Pieces, Book I* (Schotts GA, 4a and 4b) – easy.

Carcassi, *54 Selected Pieces, Book II* (Schotts GA) – medium.

Carulli, *18 Very Easy Pieces, Opus 333* (Schotts GA, 67).

Giuliani, *18 Progressive Pieces, Opus 51* (Schotts GA, 63).

Sor, *20 Selected Minuets* (Schotts GA, 15).

There are many other works by these composers and others of varying difficulty; these are suggestions to start off with. The albums are a more economical buy as they contain a good selection of works of the principal composers.

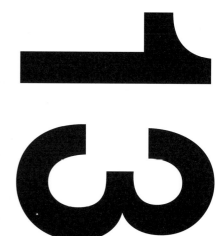

a sense of rhythm

In this chapter you will learn:

- note values

- beats and bars

- time signatures

- how to count.

▶ Note values

If you sing any song, you will hear how some notes are long and others short. If you then glance through any piece of music, you will soon notice that the characters of the notes differ considerably; some are black, some white, some have stalks, some are joined up. These differences show the different lengths of time the notes are sustained.

The diagram overleaf shows you what the notes look like, their names and lengths, and their relationship to one another. Notes worth half a beat or less can be joined or separate.

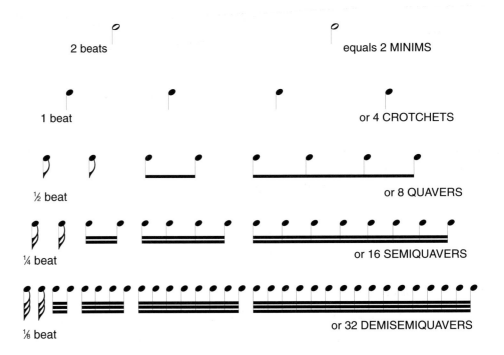

4 beats   1 SEMIBREVE

2 beats   equals 2 MINIMS

1 beat   or 4 CROTCHETS

½ beat   or 8 QUAVERS

¼ beat   or 16 SEMIQUAVERS

⅛ beat   or 32 DEMISEMIQUAVERS

Dotted notes

If a dot is placed *aft*er a note, it makes that note half its own length again.

𝅝· = 𝅝 + 𝅗𝅥 = 4 + 2 = 6 beats

𝅗𝅥· = 𝅗𝅥 + 𝅘𝅥 = 2 + 1 = 3 beats

𝅘𝅥· = 𝅘𝅥 + 𝅘𝅥𝅮 = 1 + 1½ = 1½ beats

𝅘𝅥𝅮· = 𝅘𝅥𝅮 + 𝅘𝅥𝅯 = ½ + ¼ = ¾ beat

𝅘𝅥𝅯· = 𝅘𝅥𝅯 + 𝅘𝅥𝅰 = ¼ + ⅛ = ⅜ beat

Tied notes

If two or more notes of the *same pitch* are linked together with a curved line, this is called a *tie* or *bind*. The first note only is played, but the sound is sustained for the length of all succeeding notes.

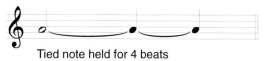

Tied note held for 4 beats

Rests

You will probably notice that there are other symbols which do not look like any of the notes. These are rests and denote a length of time when you do not play. Each note has an equivalent rest. Rests can also be dotted.

Beats and bars

All classical music has a regular rhythmic pulse like a heart-beat. For instance, a waltz has a regular *one*, two, three rhythm, while a march goes *one*, two, *one*, two. These regular accents are called beats and they form the rhythmic structure of music. The regular groups of beats such as the *one*, two, three of the waltz are called *bars*, which are marked on the stave with a line called a *bar line*:

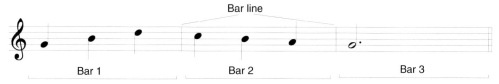

The characteristic rhythm of a piece of music is made by the accent of certain beats in the bar.

2 beats in a bar:

1	2		1	2
STRONG	weak	/	STRONG	weak

3 beats in a bar:

1	2	3		1	2	3
STRONG	weak	weak	/	STRONG	weak	weak

4 beats in a bar:

1	2	3	4		1	2	3	4
STRONG	weak	Moderate	weak	/	STRONG	weak	Moderate	weak

How to count the beats

If you add up the beats of the notes in bar 1 and then in bar 2 of the example above, you will see that they add up to the same number, 3. This means that there are three beats in each bar, some notes being subdivided, as in the first two beats of bar 3 where there are four half-beats or quavers, and some notes being sustained for more than one beat, as in the first note of bar 2 which is a minim and therefore held for two beats. The easiest way to time the length of the notes is to count the beats themselves, counting the half-beats (the quavers) between as 'and':

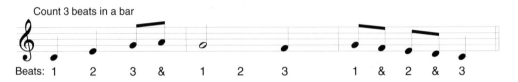

Obviously the quavers will be played twice as fast as the crotchets and the crotchets twice as fast as the minims.

Try clapping the rhythm of the tune above, counting the beats at the same time. You need not actually say 'first, second', etc., just 'one, two, three' and so on. Remember that it is essential to keep the beats rhythmically even, like the ticking of a clock.

Here are the first five bars of *God Save the Queen*:

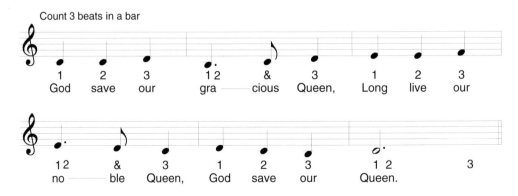

The rhythm of the word 'gracious' is long on the first syllable and short on the second. This is shown by a dotted crotchet followed by a quaver. To count this, again count the beats; the first beat is on the crotchet, the second beats starts on the dot (which, being half the length of the crotchet, is worth half a beat) and ends on the quaver (which makes up the second half of the beat).

This dotted rhythm appears again on the word 'noble'.

If there is a rest in the bar, do not forget to count that in as well:

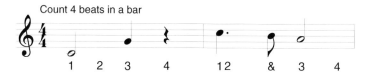

Frequently, music starts on an 'upbeat', when the first bar seems to be too short. In this case, count a full bar, playing the first note of the music on the appropriate beat. The first strong beat will fall on the first beats of the second bar. The amount of beats short in the first bar is always made up in the last bar of the piece.

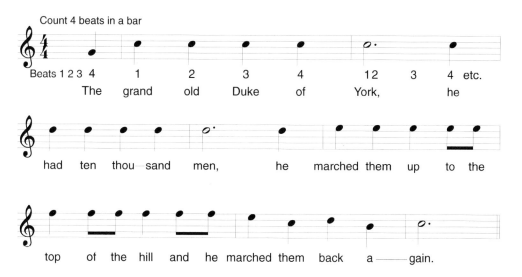

This method of starting ensures that the important words fall on the first beat of every bar, which is always the strongest or accented beat of the bar.

Time signatures

You will have noticed at the beginning of the last two musical examples two numbers like a fraction without the dividing line. This is called the *time signature*, and it describes the number and type of beats in each bar.

$\frac{3}{4}$ The top number describes how many beats there are in a bar.
The bottom number shows what kind of beats they are.

$\frac{3}{2}$ Three MINIM beats in a bar.

$\frac{3}{4}$ Three CROTCHET beats in a bar.

$\frac{3}{8}$ Three QUAVER beats in a bar.

The top numbers you will see most often at first will be 2, 3 and 4. A slightly more complicated time signature is $\frac{6}{8}$ (six quavers in a bar), described below.

Simple and compound time

If each beat in the bar can be divided equally into two smaller ones, the music is said to be in *simple time*.

Simple time signatures

$\frac{2}{2}$ is also known as *alla breve* and is sometimes written like this: ¢. $\frac{4}{4}$ is also known as *common time* and is sometimes written like this: C.

If each beat can be divided into three, the music is said to be in *compound time*. For instance:

This is called *compound duple* time because there are two dotted crotchets in a bar, each of which can be divided into three quavers, thus making a compound or mixture of two long beats, each of which has three little beats.

If there are three dotted beats in a bar, it is *compound triple* time:

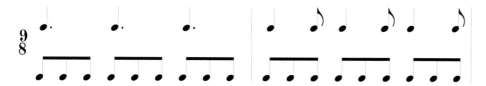

The difference between $\frac{3}{4}$ and $\frac{6}{8}$ time can be seen clearly by the way in which the notes are grouped into beats:

Although the note values are the same, the rhythmic effect is different. Try clapping each rhythm.

Triplets

Triplets are a way of varying the rhythm of a piece by playing three notes in the time it normally takes to play two notes of the same value. It is rather as if a beat of $\frac{6}{8}$ time had been introduced to a bar of simple time. A triplet is marked with a curved line and a number 3 in italics.

It is very important to count each triplet as *one whole beat*; the rhythm can best be illustrated by the nursery rhyme *Hickory Dickory Dock*:

Remember there must be a regular one, two beat throughout.

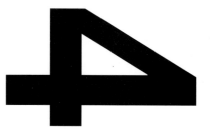

first problems

In this chapter you will learn:

- how to play barrées.

Barrée playing

Sometimes the first finger has to stop more than one string at once. This is called a barrée. The first finger lies flat across the necessary number of strings and presses them down, helped by the thumb behind. At first, the notes made often buzz, but the muscles in the hand will develop until barrées become easy.

figure 20

figure 21

Try to keep the first finger joint bent and the hand as close to the side of the fingerboard as possible, so that the hand forms a kind of clamp. Do not let your second finger rest on top of your first finger, helping to press it down; this can happen quite inadvertently, but your barrée playing will never improve and it will become a positive disadvantage when trying to play other notes in the chord (see Figure 20).

When you are playing a 'grand barrée' (see Figure 21) – in other words a six-string barrée – you may well find that the second and third strings do not sound. Sometimes it helps to place a finger a little on one side rather than flat across the fingerboard. However, the best remedy is to develop the muscles, which takes time and practice, so do not despair.

Barrées are indicated in the music by a bracket:

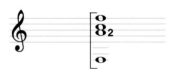

or by the letter C and the appropriate fret number:

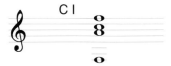

1/2 C I: Barrée over 3 strings only

Suggested easy studies for left hand

Barrée playing

Sor, *20 Studies for Guitar*, edited by Segovia: No. V (Augener-Galliard).
Carcassi, *25 Melodious and Progressive Studies*, *Opus 60*: No. 16 (Schotts GA, 2).
Giuliani, *24 Studies, Opus 100*: No. 5 (Schotts GA).

Stretching the hand

Sor, *Opus 29:* No. 20 *Tempo di Menuetto* (Schotts GA, 78).

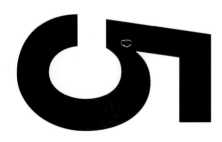

enriching the sound

> In this chapter you will learn:
>
> • how to play glissando and vibrato
>
> • how to create different tone colour.

▶ Glissando

This is a charming effect obtained by making the string sound when sliding up or down it in order to connect two notes. It is done by retaining the pressure of the finger after playing the notes whilst sliding. Care must be taken not to slide away from the note too quickly so that only half a note is played. A glissando is usually marked by the word *gliss.* and a straight line above the two notes to be joined.

Vibrato

This is a characteristic technique of all stringed instruments. A note is sustained and enriched by pressing really hard and shaking the finger from side to side in the same direction as the string; you will probably have to release your thumb in order to get enough freedom of movement. It is not a good idea to attempt vibrato until your left-hand technique is quite accurate. The best vibrato is found in the middle registers of the guitar; the lower frets are too near the nut for the string to vibrate sufficiently.

Tone colour

By now you will have experimented with the range of tone you can produce. If you play nearer the bridge you will get a much harsher tone; if you play nearer the bridge the sound will be much fuller. Similarly, you can use your fingernails to effect: more nail will make a thinner, more assertive tone. Tone colour is dealt with fully on the CD.

Try playing this piece by yourself, experimenting with tone colour.

Arietta

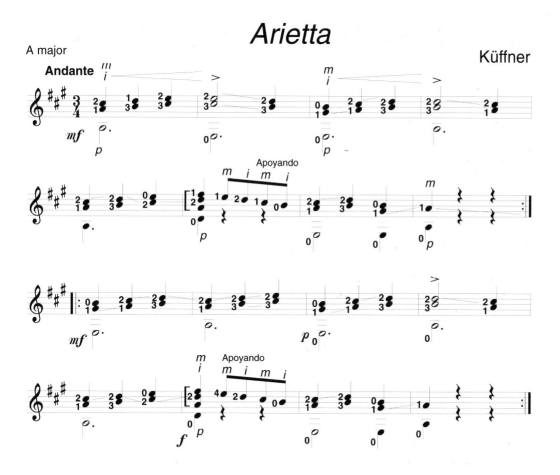

understanding keys

In this chapter you will learn:

- the construction of major and minor scales

- keys and key signatures

- technical names of the notes of the scale.

Construction of major scales

By now you should be practising scales regularly and have learnt to identify the characteristic sounds of the major and minor keys. Their own particular sounds are formed by the distribution of the tones and semitones.

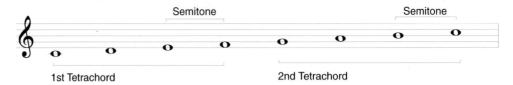

The first octave of the scale of C major can be divided into two groups of four notes, each group being called a *tetrachord*. The interval between the third and fourth notes of each tetrachord is a semitone; the interval between each of the other notes is a tone.

The second of the two tetrachords can now be used to form the first tetrachord of the scale of G major:

1st Tetrachord   2nd Tetrachord

However, in order to keep the characteristic 'major' sound, the third note of the second tetrachord has to be raised a semitone to F♯ to make the interval between the third and fourth notes only a semitone.

Remember, then, that the semitones in a major scale fall between the third and fourth and the seventh and eighth notes of the octave and in order to ensure this all major scales, apart from C major, will need additional sharps or flats as the case may be. These sharps or flats are grouped together at the beginning of the scale, immediately after the clef, and are called the *key signature*. They are written in an invariable order illustrated below. The first note of the scale is called the *key note*.

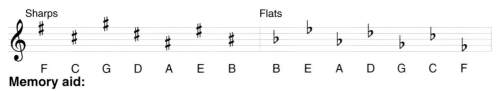

Memory aid:

　　Fat　Cook　Goes　Down　And　Eats　Bread.
The flats are the reverse order.

Key signatures

	Key	Sharps	Flats		Key
C	major	0	0	C	major
G	major	1	1	F	major
D	major	2	2	B♭	major
A	major	3	3	E♭	major
E	major	4	4	A♭	major
B	major	5	5	D♭	major
F♯	major	6	6	G♭	major
C♯	major	7			

Key signatures never contain a mixture of sharps and flats, only one or the other.

The scale of G♭ is usually written in the enharmonic F♯ and, similarly, the scale of D♭ is usually written in the enharmonic C♯.

Any additional accidentals are written in the music. An accidental lasts for the duration of one bar only and is cancelled out by the bar line. It is only written once in a bar but is 'understood' for other notes on the same bar of the same pitch.

Construction of minor scales

The last three notes of a major scale form the first three notes of its *relative minor* scale – that is to say, the minor scale with the same key signature.

When comparing the first tetrachord of A minor with the first tetrachord of A major, you can see that the semitone in the minor scale falls between the second and third notes instead of between the third and fourth notes as in the major scale. The crucial note is the third note, which decides whether a scale is major or minor.

The interval from the key note to the third note in a minor scale is composed of three semitones; the interval from the key note to the third note in a major scale is composed of four semitones. The word 'major' means greater and the word 'minor' lesser.

There are two ways of writing the second tetrachord in a minor scale. One way is to sharpen the seventh note, thus forming intervals of a semitone between the fifth and sixth and the seventh and eighth notes of the scale, and a large gap of three semitones between the sixth and seventh notes:

This type of minor scale is called a *harmonic* minor scale.

The other type of minor scale is the *melodic* minor, so named because it is much smoother and easier to sing since the big gap between the sixth and seventh notes is eliminated. The sixth and seventh notes are raised a semitone in the ascending scale but are lowered again in the descending scale in order to keep the smoothness and also to retain the minor 'sound', which otherwise does not return until the third note (C♮).

In the minor scales, the accidentals introduced into the scale (i.e. the sharpened and flattened sixth and seventh notes) are written in the scale and are not included in the key signature.

If the seventh note is already sharpened, e.g. F♯ in G♯ minor, the note is raised a further semitone by using a double sharp, ✗. In a scale it is essential to have a note on every line and in every space, so that it is necessary to write F✗ rather than G♯. For the same reason, it is sometimes necessary to use a ♭♭.

Remember that relative keys are major and minor keys sharing the same key signature. A relative minor key can be found by counting down three semitones from the major key note, and the procedure reversed to find a relative major key.

Key signatures

	Key		Sharps		Flats		Key	
	A	minor	0		0		A	minor
	E	minor	1		1		D	minor
	B	minor	2		2		G	minor
	F♯	minor	3		3		C	minor
	C♯	minor	4		4		F	minor
	G♯	minor	5		5		B♭	minor
	D♯	minor	6	enharmonic	6		E♭	minor
	A♯	minor	7		7		A♭	minor

Technical names

The technical names for the notes of the scale describe the position of the notes in the scale and their relationship to each other.

1st note	Doh	*Tonic.* The key note (note tone) from which the scale takes its name.
2nd note	Ray	*Super tonic.* The note immediately after the tonic.
3rd note	Me	*Mediant.* The note midway between the first and fifth notes.
4th note	Fah	*Subdominant.* The note positioned four notes above the tonic: the same distance as the fifth note lies below the tonic.
5th note	Soh	*Dominant.* Second only in importance to the tonic and so dominates the key.
6th note	Lah	*Submediant.* The note midway between the tonic (doh) and the subdominant.
7th note	Te	*Leading note.* The note leading to the tonic (doh).

This diagram shows how the notes all relate to the tonic:

understanding chords

In this chapter you will learn about:

- tonic triads and their inversions

- what cadences are.

Tonic triads and inversions

A *tonic triad* is a chord comprising three notes; the lowest note is the tonic, the middle note is the mediant and the top note is the dominant of a scale.

Tonic triad of C major

When the tonic of the scale is the lowest note of the chord, the tonic triad is said to be in *root position*.

If the mediant of the tonic triad is the lowest note of the chord and the other notes are arranged above it (in any order), it is called the *first inversion* of the tonic triad.

If the dominant of the tonic triad is the lowest note of the chord, it is called the *second inversion* of the tonic triad:

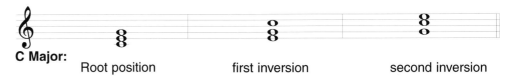

C Major: Root position   first inversion   second inversion

Remember, it is always the lowest note of the chord that describes its position. You should be able to recognise a chord in any position. Obviously, the median in the minor tonic triad will be a semitone lower than the equivalent on the major triad:

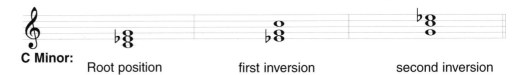

C Minor: Root position   first inversion   second inversion

A triad can be formed on any note of the scale.

Cadences

A piece of music is made up of musical phrases, each one leading towards a kind of ending or climax. These endings are called *cadences*.

Cadences are a form of musical punctuation. Certain chord sequences give a sense of repose or finality, like a full stop; others give the feeling of something yet to come, like a semicolon. The important notes to listen to are the bass notes, which show which chords are being used. The chords are either named by the technical name of the bass note from which the chord is formed (tonic, dominant, etc.) or described by a Roman numeral indicating its position in the scale (I, V, etc.).

Perfect cadence (full close). Dominant to tonic or V.I.

Plagal cadence (nicknamed the 'Amen' cadence). Subdominant to tonic or IV.I.

Both these cadences have a feeling of finality about them; the following, although representing a moment of rest, feel as if they want to move on.

Imperfect cadence (half close). Tonic to dominant or I.V., or subdominant to dominant or IV.V.

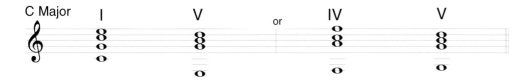

Interrupted cadence. Dominant to submediant or V.VI.

C Major

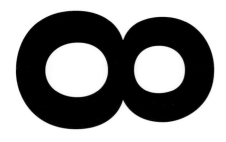

musical shorthand

In this chapter you will learn about:

• ornaments, arpeggios, signs and symbols.

There are a number of signs and symbols in music which have to be memorised as they refer specifically to, or directly affect, the performance of a piece.

Ornaments

An ornament is a group of notes used to decorate a melody note. In the seventeenth and eighteenth centuries, the decoration of a note was left to the performer to improvise according to musical traditions. However, the ornaments most in use today are indicated by signs. They are: the turn, the appoggiatura, the acciaccatura, the mordent and the trill.

The turn

The turn consists of a group of four notes played either instead of or after the note above which the sign ∾ is written. The notes are: the note above, the note itself, the note below and the note itself.

Written:

Played:

A sharp or flat placed above or below the sign refers to the notes above or below the original note:

Written:

Played:

The appoggiatura

The appoggiatura, or leading note, is a small note written immediately before the principal note and receives half its value:

Written:

Played:

If it is placed before a dotted note, it receives two thirds of the value of that note:

Written:

Played:

The acciaccatura

The acciaccatura, or crushing note, is a small note written immediately before the principal note and is played as quickly as possible on the beat. It differs in appearance from the appoggiatura in that it is written invariably as a quaver with a line through it:

Written:

Played:

The mordent

There are two types of mordent: the upper and the inverted. *The upper mordent* consists of three notes: the principal note, the note above and the principal note again played as fast as possible in the time of the principal note.

Written: Played:

The inverted mordent is played in the same way, except that the three notes are the principal note, the lower note and the principal note again.

Written: Played:

An accidental placed above or below the mordent sign refers to the note above or below the principal note.

The trill

The trill or shake is the rapid alternation of the written note and the note above it. The number of alternations depends on the length of the principal note and the speed of the music. The trill usually ends with a turn.

Written:

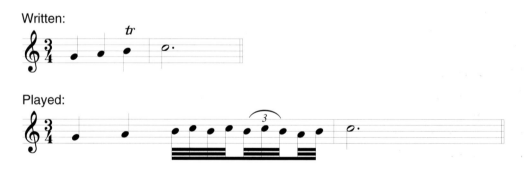

Played:

In music of the period up to and including Mozart, the trill normally starts on the upper note.

Arpeggios

Arpeggios are a way of playing a chord. Instead of playing the notes of the chord simultaneously, they are played like an arpeggio (see page 12).

Written: Played:

Repeat signs

Repeated passages are marked by a double bar line at the beginning and end, with two dots on the right side of the first double bar line and on the left of the second. The section between is repeated. If the repeated passage starts at the beginning of the piece of music, there are only double dotted bar lines at the end of the section.

Sometimes there are two endings to the repeated section. In this case, the ending marked 1 is played the first time and omitted on the repeat, when the ending marked 2 is played.

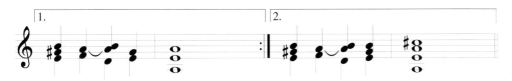

Da capo, abbreviated D.C., means repeat from the beginning.

Dal segno, abbreviated D.S., means repeat from the sign 𝄋. In this case, the end is usually shown by the word *fine*, meaning 'the end'.

Repeated notes

When a note is to be repeated rapidly within one bar, it is marked by a line through the stem. One line indicates quaver repetition, two lines semiquaver, and so on. A similar sign is used for rapidly alternating notes within the bar.

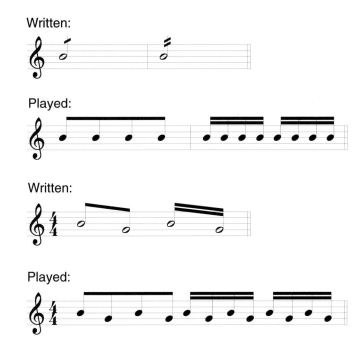

Expression marks

Apart from the many Italian words indicating the speed, volume and mood of a piece (see Glossary), there are also symbols relating to the performance:

Phrase mark: indicating a group of notes that should be linked together in sound. Not to be confused with slurring (see Chapter 20).

Pause: can be over a note or rest; the length of time it is held for is determined by the character of the piece. A note is usually sustained by vibrato.

These notes are played one octave above the written pitch.

These notes are to be played one octave below the written pitch.

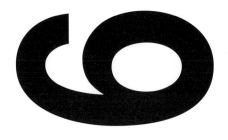

advanced techniques for the right hand

In this chapter you will learn:

• how to play tremolo, pizzicato, rasgueado, percussion and golpe.

After you have been playing some simple pieces for some time, you will no doubt want to branch out into more ambitious repertoire. You will find when glancing through the music that there are certain passages which you either do not understand or which seem particularly difficult. These often need certain specialised techniques, which either are indicated in the music by signs or are immediately recognisable. Many of these techniques are borrowed from Flamenco music.

▶ Tremolo

Tremolo is one of the most difficult techniques to perfect but also one of the most rewarding. The word means 'a trembling, a shaking' and is easily recognised by the rapid repetitive top note. A famous example of tremolo is *Recuerdos de la Alhambra* by Tarrega:

Tarrega: *Recuerdos de la Alhambra*
etc.

Each beat is divided into four notes, the thumb playing the base note followed by *ami* repeating the top note.

One of the main difficulties is to get the tremolo even; a common fault is to play the third finger too quickly after the thumb. Metronome practice is invaluable for correcting this, especially if the metronome is set to beat time on the first and third notes of each quaver beat.

You will find that you will need to keep your right-hand thumb nearer your fingers than in arpeggio playing and your wrist higher, so that your fingers can vibrate the strings with the minimum movement and the maximum speed. A perfect tremolo sounds like a ripple.

A good study to learn for your first attempt at tremolo is *Allegro*, *Opus 60*, No. 7, by Carcassi.

Pizzicato

Pizzicato is a right-hand technique used to make very short notes, providing another interesting tone contrast. It is usually marked in the music by the abbreviation *Pizz*.

figure 22

There are two ways of playing pizzicato; in both cases the right hand stays very close to the bridge. One way is to use the thumb, keeping the hand slightly flatter than usual and stopping the string with the thumb immediately after it has been played. The other method is to use the whole hand, keeping the thumb stiff and playing the hand and thumb as one unit; that is, not swinging the thumb up when it sounds the string but moving the hand and thumb together and then quickly stopping the string with the side of the hand and thumb (see Figure 22). The first method tends to produce a more muted tone, the second a rather sharper tone. You must decide which is the most effective for the passage concerned.

Rasgueado

Rasgueado is a Flamenco technique occasionally used for playing chords. The right-hand fingers bend under into the palm of the hand and strum the strings as they straighten out again (see Figure 23). They hit the strings in the order *ami* and move so quickly that you cannot hear the different fingers hitting the strings.

figure 23

Percussion

This is a method of sounding the strings with the right-hand thumb by beating the strings with the side of the thumb very near the bridge. The resulting sound is very muted but rather effective in some Spanish pieces.

Golpe

This means to hit. The right-hand thumb is held lengthwise above the bridge and hits or knocks it sharply (see Figure 24).

figure 24

advanced techniques for the left hand

In this chapter you will learn:

• how to play slurs

• how to play harmonics.

▶ Slurring

Slurring is a left-hand technique used either for playing very fast notes, such as in an ornament or a fast run, or when you want to play more than one note on the same string, such as an arpeggio movement. The slurred notes are played and sounded by the *left hand* only, and are indicated in the music by a curved line like this:

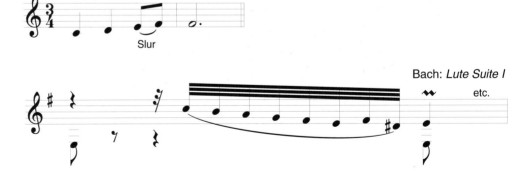

A long fast run where all the notes are slurred

Slurring an ascending note(s) in a scale passage

When the notes to be slurred are ascending, the first note under the slur sign is *struck* in the normal way by the right hand, and any subsequent notes in the slur are *hit* and thus sounded by the left-hand fingers only; the right hand only sounds the struck note and rests during the other notes.

S = struck note with right hand

The action of the left-hand fingers can be likened to a hammering movement, as if you were trying to hammer nails into the fingerboard with your fingers. It is essential that the fingers hit the strings (i) in the same place as they would when stopping the strings and (ii) absolutely on the finger *tips*, otherwise a muzzy tone will result. The fingers only make the movement, not the hand. To get the correct movement, you must keep your fingers bent and your hand parallel to the fingerboard (see Figure 25a). Do not let your hand slip round at an angle to the fingerboard, otherwise you will slur with a straight finger (see Figure 25b).

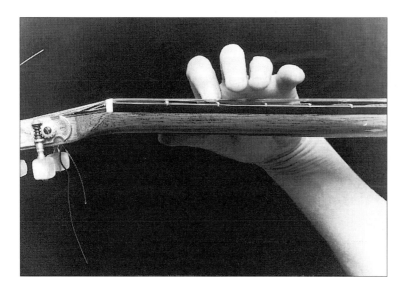

figure 25a

The tone quality of a slurred note should be as strong and clear as a played note; only long, slow practice will teach you the movement and strengthen your fingers. Your first attempt might well result in total silence!

figure 25b

Slurring a descending note(s)

When slurring a passage of descending notes, the first note included in the slur sign is struck by the right hand (as before) and any other subsequent notes are hooked off and thus sounded by the left hand only. The finger tip actually hooks the string upwards in as near a vertical movement as possible, and the string sounds when it is released. The important thing to remember is that the finger hooks upwards and does not merely pull the string backwards towards the adjacent string: this movement distorts the sound, because the string is pulled out of its natural line, and there is also the risk of touching the other string and the slurred string, thus killing the sound.

Slurring an ornament

Normally *all* notes in an ornament, apart from the first struck note, are slurred, even though the notes will ascend and descend, due to the speed needed to fit all the notes in.

Scarlatti: *Sonata in E Minor*

Slurring an arpeggio

It is necessary to slur a six-note arpeggio if more than one note falls on the same string. Slurring the appropriate notes will make the arpeggio far smoother and easier to play.

Tarrega: *Scherzo*

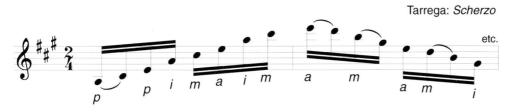

You will notice that the right hand does not in this case play apoyando but tirando, as in any arpeggio or broken-chord playing. Sometimes the thumb plays more than one note consecutively; in this case, the sound is more connected if the thumb falls straight onto the next string instead of playing each string individually. If the thumb is playing more than one note but they are separated by a slurred note, you must be careful not to touch the slurred string or the sound will be killed.

Suggested studies

Sor, *20 Studies*: No. XI (Augener-Galliard).
Tarrega, *Scherzo-Estudio in A* (Biblioteca Fortea).
Giuliani, *24 Studies, Opus 48*: Nos. 4 & 11 (Schotts GA, 32).
Giuliani, *Studies for Phrasing and Ornamentation* (Schotts GA, 31).

Harmonics

Harmonics are a natural sound effect made by vibrating a fraction of the string instead of the whole length. The harmonics are made by touching the string lightly at specified points; this stops the whole length vibrating and leaves only a section to vibrate. The sound produced is very clear and resonant, and sustains for some time after the note has been played. Harmonics are normally used only for special effects, such as a sudden contrast, or a kind of musical exclamation mark.

There are two ways of playing harmonics: *natural* harmonics, which are played on open strings, and *artificial* harmonics, which are played on stopped strings.

Natural harmonics

Natural harmonics are made by sounding the string with the right hand whilst touching the strings lightly with the left hand. As only a fraction of the string vibrates, the harmonic pitch is not the same as the note produced by stopping the strings at the same places. The most commonly played harmonics are on the fifth, seventh and twelfth frets.

Harmonics are shown in the music in several different ways. One of the most common is to use 'lozenges'.

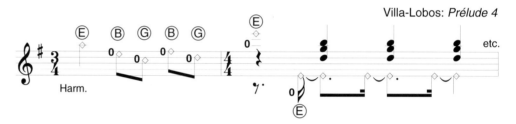

The harmonic is most often written at the pitch where it is played rather than at the pitch that actually sounds. In the example above, the strings are named as an aid; it is quite common to name the fret as well:

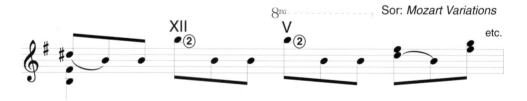

The method of touching the string with the left hand has to be very accurate. The fingers must be kept quite straight and almost stiff, and must touch the string directly above, and laying parallel to, the fret. The easiest harmonics to play are those on the twelfth fret, and you should experiment with them until you find the exact pressure to put on the string.

The right hand should play apoyando or tirando, depending on the context, in the same way as usual. However, it should play much nearer the bridge.

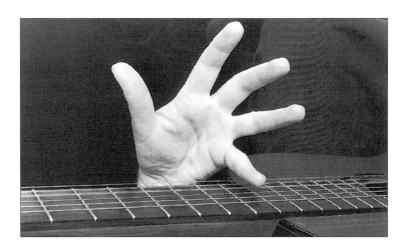

figure 26

Artificial harmonics

Artificial harmonics are made principally by the right hand. The left hand stops the notes in the normal way, which sound in harmonics one octave higher. The right hand has to touch the string lightly with the forefinger (*i*) and simultaneously

figure 27

sound the string with the third finger (*a*). Obviously these are much harder to play than natural harmonics, particularly as finger *a* has to be very strong to be able to bend back and sound the string.

The right hand touches the string an octave higher than the stopped note: for example, if the stopped note is F, first fret, first string, the right-hand forefinger would have to touch the *same* string on the thirteenth fret. It is useful to use the twelfth fret as a guide; the harmonic lies the same number of frets above the twelfth fret as the stopped note lies above the nut.

Pieces containing examples of harmonics

Natural: *Prélude 4* by Villa-Lobos (Max Eschig).
Artificial: *El Testamen de N'Amelia* arranged by Llobet (Biblioteca Fortea).

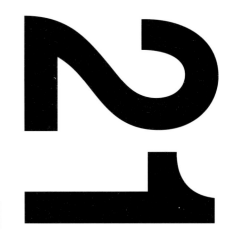

fingering

In this chapter you will learn:

• how to finger a more complicated passage.

Examples and suggestions of how to finger a new piece

An essential part of guitar playing, and one of the most difficult skills to acquire, is how to finger a piece of music really satisfactorily. One of the main problems is that you must always think ahead to what is coming next in order to make the transition from one chord to another as smooth and as easy as possible. Obviously experience is by far the most valuable asset, as you will get to know certain musical clichés and remember certain movements from previous pieces of music.

Everybody develops their own idiosyncrasies in actually marking the music; for instance, I like to ring the appropriate right-hand fingers to remind me to put them in the strings simultaneously, and also to mark which notes are to be played apoyando and which tirando. Different people use different right-hand symbols; you will notice how they differ in printed music.

When you have been playing for some time, do not be afraid to question the fingerings given in the music and to alter them if you can think of a better way of playing that particular sequence. Remember that you can play many notes in more than one place, getting a different sound effect in each place: for instance, the sound of an open E is quite different from E played on the third string on the ninth fret, although they are the same in pitch. You must listen carefully to the sounds and decide which is more suitable or effective for that particular passage.

Always look for chord patterns, or sequences as they are known; the fingers can soon learn a pattern and it will be easier to play. If you have a scale passage, your scale practice should help you to finger it. However, you must be aware of the context of the passage and be ready to adapt the fingering if necessary.

It is essential that you check the fingering of a piece before you learn it, otherwise you could cause yourself hours of unnecessary practice on a difficult passage which only needs an alternative and more straightforward fingering. Really difficult music, such as a Bach suite, takes many hours of patient work, but it is well worth the effort.

Points to remember

Left hand

One of the most obvious difficulties in fingering the left hand is finding how to get from one chord to the next smoothly and easily. The first thing to look for is a finger that can slide to one of the notes in the next chord. If there is one, mark it with a straight line and, if necessary, also mark the fret.

Carcassi: *Caprice 1*
etc.

In the example shown above, there is also an × marked. This is to show that the second and third fingers cross in the air whilst the first finger is sliding, thus changing strings. These 'cross movements' are very useful but need to be practised thoroughly to get them fast and neat.

Try to find the patterns. The rather unnerving passage overleaf is made easy by sliding all the fingers all the time, so that the dramatic quality of the passage stands out.

Villa-Lobos: *Prélude 1*

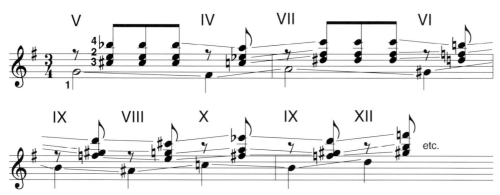

In the following sequence where the original phrase is repeated in descending semitones, a finger pattern simplifies the whole thing. Without a pattern, the passage would be harder to play and could sound very laboured.

Sor: *Estudio XVI*

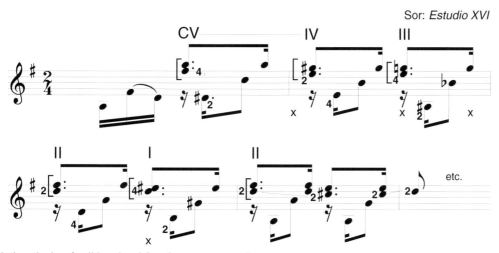

Each time the barrée slides, 4 and 2 make a × movement

You must be able to play a chord or scale in as many different ways as possible. One of the dangers of chord books is that they tend to fix the chord in the memory in an invariable position. This is far from true. For example, the chord of D major can be played in at least three ways, as follows:

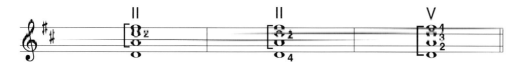

Scales are also versatile. For instance, you could play the following scale here:

or here:

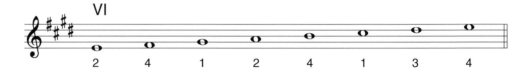

The effect is completely different and is particularly useful when there is a repeated section that needs contrast.

In the following example, the piece starts in the second position and the repeat starts in the seventh position, giving a warmer, richer sound:

Bach: *Gavotte*

Do not take off fingers that might come in useful later on. In the following passage, the third finger stays on for seven beats:

Carcassi: *Allegro*

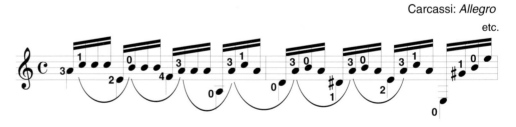

Occasionally you will see the words '6me en Re'. This means that the sixth string is tuned down a tone to D, and consequently all notes on this string are stopped a tone higher than normal. It is often found in lute transcriptions, as the lute is tuned a tone lower than the guitar.

Dowland: *Dowland's Adew*

Right hand

The principal concern is tirando or apoyando? Chords and arpeggios are always played tirando, with the exception of the top note of an arpeggio which is occasionally played apoyando, in this case to make a slur.

Villa-Lobos: *Prélude 2*

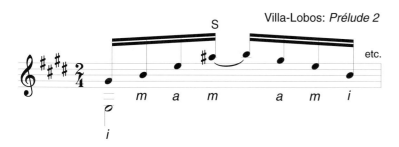

Apoyando is rather more complicated, and it is useful to mark these notes, as I have above, with an S (for strike). As a general rule, apoyando is used for single-note passages, but in the following slurred passage the right hand is played tirando between the slurs:

Villa-Lobos: *Prélude 2*

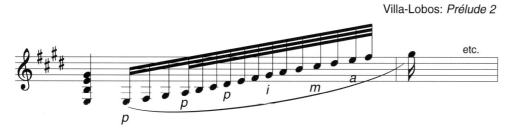

The right hand has to be careful not to play apoyando if the finger will fall back on a sustained note. This is particularly important in contrapuntal music, when a line of music will be broken.

Thomas Robinson: *Gigue*

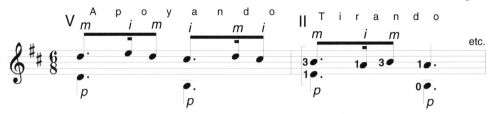

Bar 1 is played apoyando. Bar 2 is played tirando because the bass E would be stopped

A run of struck notes must be carefully fingered so that string changing is easy and any subsequent chords can be added.

Bach: *Lute Suite I – Prélude*

By starting the apoyando run with *m*, the other fingers in the chord fall onto the right strings

Remember to alternate the fingers, particularly in *pi*, *pm* passages. This keeps the fingers from tiring, and the tone clear and even.

Carcassi: *Caprice 4*

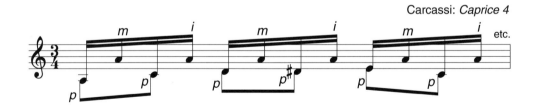

If the piece has a melody on the top string, care must be taken not to touch the string until the last possible moment when the note changes. In such a case, the left hand must also sustain the pressure.

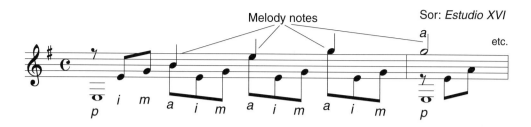

Melody notes

Sor: *Estudio XVI*

If the notes are to be played *legato*, in other words in a smooth and connected manner, the appropriate fingers must be put in the strings together before they are played off. Again, it is helpful to mark this.

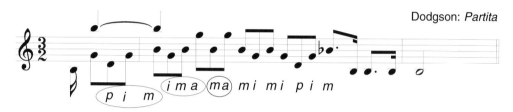

Dodgson: *Partita*

Do not be afraid to mark everything in the manuscript; you will learn the piece far quicker because you will use the same fingering each time you practise.

communication

In this chapter you will learn about:

• phrasing and interpretation.

Playing an instrument does not end with getting the notes out accurately; on the contrary, this is the point where the music begins. A piece of music is often compared to a conversation where notes are used instead of words to express an idea. As with speech, the phrasing and emphasis put upon some notes, and the speed with which they are played, bring out the meaning of the piece. For example, take the simple sentence: 'I like red apples.' Try saying it aloud, emphasising each word in turn, and see how the meaning of the sentence is altered:

> *I* like red apples.
> I *like* red apples.
> I like *red* apples.
> I like red *apples*.

In the same way that you make yourself understood by deliberately controlling your intonation, you must control the way you play a note in order to give meaning to a piece of music.

Phrasing

Phrasing is a way of dividing the music into 'sentences', some more important than others. You must decide which phrases build up to a climax and 'colour' them accordingly: by tempo, dynamic or tonal quality, or by a mixture of all three. In the case of a crescendo or a diminuendo, do not fall into the trap of leaving the dynamic change until the last few notes unless specifically instructed; the overall effect should be one of building up or dying away.

Bach: *Lute Suite III*

Phrases frequently cross bar lines; in this case, you must think through to the end of the phrase rather than rigidly chop up the line of music into bars.

Dodgson: *Partita*

etc.

The beginning of a phrase can be marked by slightly accenting the first note, or by taking a slight 'breath' or making a small hesitation before the first note. However, not all phrases warrant such strong definition and are 'felt' rather than forcibly marked.

Phrasing is an art; it is instinctive as well as cerebral. It is always worth listening to the great performers to hear how they approach such subtleties.

Interpretation

The best performer is really a medium, acting as a link between the composer and the audience. Obviously his own personality will affect his interpretation, but the performer is always secondary to the composer. Thus interpreting a piece of music is far from being wholly emotional as some people think; indeed, many hours of thought go into a performance, apart from the hours of practice. In early works, that is up to and including Bach, there are also technical problems of interpretation, such as the ornaments, which need factual knowledge and often research.

When playing a piece, one of the most important considerations is the tempo. Bach's *Air on a G String* would hardly sound the same at three times the pace and the *William Tell Overture* would lose all its excitement at half speed. Metronome speeds are usually taken as an appropriate guide, although some contemporary works do give very definite speeds or time limits. The most important guide is the Italian word at the beginning of a piece of music describing the tempo. There are a number of these going through all the gradations from *Largo*, meaning broadly, slowly, stately, to *Prestissimo*, meaning as fast as possible, and they all have to be memorised (see Glossary).

Many pieces do not have to be kept to an exact tempo throughout, much the same as a conversation changes pace. Sometimes this is indicated by an Italian term: *Accelerando*, meaning getting gradually faster; *Ritardando*, meaning getting gradually slower. Sometimes, though, you feel instinctively that the pace needs to slacken off or broaden out, for instance when approaching a perfect cadence. However, any adjustment of the speed should be made within the framework of the basic tempo, otherwise it will become meaningless.

The dynamics of a composition – that is to say, how loudly it is played – are also of great importance; the difference in the emotional effect of very loud and moderately loud is enormous. Dynamics are also indicated by Italian expressions. The guitar, compared, for example, with the piano, is a quiet instrument, without a very wide range of dynamics. However, what it does have, and what is to my mind one of its principal beauties and subtleties, is an exquisite and subtle range of nuance in the tone colouring: by moving the right hand slightly nearer to or farther away from the bridge, a different quality of harshness or mellowness of tone is produced, which is where the expensive and more responsive instruments prove their worth. It takes many hours of practice to get full control of the different inflections of tone, and you should always strive to improve your tone in richness and variety. Of course, there are also the special techniques such as pizzicato (see Chapter 19) which can be employed to good effect.

Style is another important aspect of interpretation. All the main periods of music have their own characteristic sound, and so do the principal composers within those periods, which should be instantly recognisable. Through listening to music and studying musical history and form, you should be able to grasp and communicate the different styles of composition.

A good technique is essential for playing and interpreting a piece of music; the turn of a phrase, the approach to a cadence are dependent on the confidence and security of your fingers.

practising

In this chapter you will learn:

- how to practise selectively

- what technical practice you must do

- how to develop your sight reading

- which mechanical aids you might need.

▶ To get the greatest benefit from practising, you must do so *regularly*. This is an invaluable lesson to learn, particularly early on when everything is unfamiliar, and only frequent repetition will make the guitar seem more of an old friend and less of a frustrating stranger.

At first, it often seems impossible to fit in an hour or so's practice every day. I have found that the best idea is to set aside a certain time each day for practice and stick to this same time rigidly for about a week until it becomes part of your everyday routine. You always find time to eat, mainly because mealtimes are at more or less the same time every day. Try the same system with practising.

Selective practising

Obviously the amount of time you can set aside each day will depend on the individual, but I would suggest that after the first few months, by which time you should be working on a selection of pieces, scales and studies, you should aim at a minimum of one hour a day. The less time you have, the more you will have to condense your practice and select what you work on. A very common mistake is to sit down, play or stumble through a couple of pieces two or three times and then feel virtuous for having played for half an hour. A far more valuable method is to analyse what is making you stumble and then practise the couple of bars – or even couple of notes if they are the cause of the trouble – until the stumble is eliminated and the whole piece, as a result, sounds a hundred times better.

Sometimes it is difficult to see why the passage is causing so much trouble, particularly if it is not just downright difficult, and needs more work than the rest of the piece. It is a good idea to check first that the fingering is not at fault and that you cannot think of a simpler one that will make a smoother connection. At the same time you can check to see that you are playing the right notes and that you have not forgotten any accidentals. If there is any special movement involved, for instance a slur or a difficult chord change, learn it on its own until the fingers can make the movement automatically. The secret here is to practise as *slowly* as you can and, if possible, to memorise the passage so that you can watch your hand rather than the music and correct any faults. I cannot over-emphasise the value of slow practice; you can correct and improve your technique so that, when you come to play at speed again, your positioning will be completely accurate.

Technique – scales, arpeggios and studies

One of the most important parts of your practice routine lies in your technique, that is to say the scales, arpeggios and studies that you practise. Scales should be an automatic way of 'warming up', making your fingers supple and responsive. Remember that, apart from single-note scales, there are chromatic scales (scales played in semitones), scales in thirds, sixths and octaves, to say nothing of all the arpeggios. They are essential not only to get a feeling for the different keys but also to learn exactly how to place your fingers and how to play at speed. I have had many pupils complain about my insistence on scale practice until they realise how vital it is for playing fast. You can vary the practice by accenting the beat in different ways; for instance, you could play the scales in triplets by accenting the first of every three beats, then try the same with every four notes and later with every six. Another useful way of practising scales is by trying to get a very even crescendo on the ascending scale and a diminuendo on the descent. There are four types of arpeggio; major, formed from the notes of the tonic triad of the major scale; minor, formed from the tonic triad of the minor scale; dominant seventh, formed by the notes of the triad of the dominant chord plus the note a minor seventh from its root – for example, the arpeggio of G 7th consists of G, B, D, F; and diminished seventh, formed by any four notes each separated by a minor third. One of the chief difficulties is to get them even; you should not be able to hear any change of fret. They should sound bold, strong and rhythmical.

Studies, despite their academic title, can be very attractive and great fun to play. A collection that immediately springs to mind is the well-known twenty by Fernando Sor. It is a good idea to choose studies that are particularly relevant to the pieces you are working on at the same time. For instance, if you are working on a piece with an especially difficult slurred passage such as this:

Coste: *Étude 6*

it would be useful to back it up by practising a study such as the fourth study in Carcassi's *25 Melodious and Progressive Studies, Opus 60*.

Some studies concentrate on the left-hand technique, others on the right hand, and you must decide when you need to improve the appropriate hand. More advanced studies present problems for both hands.

Suggested scale books

Andres Segovia, *Diatonic Major and Minor Scales* (Schotts GA).

Suggested study books

Collections by: Aguado, Carcassi, Giuliani, Coste, Sor, Villa-Lobos, Legnani.

For beginners, Carcassi, *25 Melodious and Progressive Studies, Opus 60*, and Giuliani, *24 Studies, Opus 48*, both published by Schotts, are particularly recommended.

Sor wrote an enormous amount of studies, the famous twenty being the most difficult. There are many other collections as well, some very easy, some elementary and some of progressive difficulty. Do not try to run before you can walk; you will only get put off.

Sight reading

It is a very good idea to do a little sight reading every day, even if it is only a few bars. Although some people pick it up quicker than others, everyone can become a good sight reader with practice, and the advantages of being able to sight read straight through a new piece are enormous. One common fault I have noticed in beginners is a tendency to read the notes on the music and then to look at the fingerboard in order to place their fingers. This is a fatal mistake, as in this way their *fingers* never learn the notes, only their eyes. You must learn to play from music in the same way as a typist learns to touch type: by feeling the distances between the notes and their relationship to one another. At first, the temptation to look at your fingers is almost unbearable, but by starting with very simple pieces, or even a scale, it soon becomes easy. Try playing a piece that you know well, looking only at the music, so that you will start to coordinate the dots on the music with the frets on the guitar.

Another helpful aid is to read the score when listening to music, on CDs for example. In this way you will learn to identify the rise and fall of the sound with the patterns on the manuscript. Eventually you should be able to read right through quite complicated music, 'hearing' it in your head.

When trying out a completely new piece of music, there are several points to remember:

1 Look at the key signature and decide on the key. If you cannot decide if it is major or minor (e.g. G major or E minor), look at the last bar, which usually ends with the key chord.

2 Look at the time signature. If there are many divided beats in the music, it is sometimes easier to count them instead of the whole beats. For instance, $\frac{2}{4}$ could be counted as $\frac{4}{8}$.

3 Glance through the music, trying to feel the rhythm and keeping an eye open for accidentals. Decide on the right-hand movements and mark them if necessary.

4 Play *slowly*. You will get much more of an idea of the whole than if you try to 'perform' it and end up with muffed notes and hiccups.

5 In a chord change, always look for a slide or cross movement first and then read the notes from the bass note up.

Mechanical aids – metronomes, tape recorders and CDs

Metronomes are instruments rather like clocks which can be set at different speeds to 'tick' the beat of a piece of music. Most music printed now has a metronomic speed indicating the speed of performance (e.g. ♩ = 112). This means that the music should be played at a speed of 112 crotchet beats in a minute.

Metronomes can be used for practising to help to correct unevenness or to improve the speed of a passage. However, they should be used with discretion as overuse can destroy the natural feel for rhythm and can make the player sound like an automaton.

Tape recorders are invaluable for self-criticism. Use your score when listening to mark faulty passages.

CDs and cassettes are of great value for encouragement and inspiration. It is particularly interesting to have several recordings of a piece to compare the interpretation.

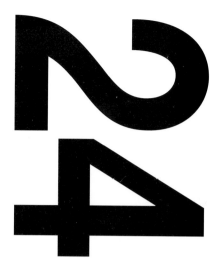

moving on

In this chapter you will learn about:

- exams and competitions

- performing and memorising.

Examinations and competitions

These depend very much on the individual and how ambitious he or she is. Examinations can be very useful inasmuch as they provide a goal to work for and force you to raise your standard of playing and musicianship all round. Competitions can be nerve-racking, but a good adjudicator will give a constructive criticism and it is always interesting to hear others play.

Performing

For most people, performing is the ultimate goal, although with varying degrees of ambition. Amateur music making can be great fun and of great value in finding out one's weak points under stress. Always play pieces that you know inside out; it is funny how one reacts when keyed up. If you are giving a recital, take a lot of time and trouble over the programme; do not jump from period to period, try to create an atmosphere. That is not to say that you should not have a good deal of variety in what you play, but group it effectively. If you do make a few mistakes, ignore them and keep going.

Memorising

Some people have a great deal of trouble memorising music, which can be rather annoying for them. First, I should like to stress that the importance of memorising can easily be overemphasised so that the student gets much more anxious about it than necessary, which makes memorising even harder.

If you decide that you really do want to memorise something (it often is not necessary), try to learn a little at a time; a few bars will do to start with. Try to learn a small amount each day, to increase the overall amount, and choose something really easy at first. You will soon find that your fingers develop a mechanical memory through the constant repetition of the same patterns. However, what very often happens is that, if concentration is broken, you are unable to pick up from where you stopped; basically, this is due to not really understanding the chord progressions. It is a very good idea to start practising from different points in the piece, both with and without the music, so that you get to know the work thoroughly. Do not try to learn too much at once, and do not push it if you are not doing too well; your memory will develop with experience.

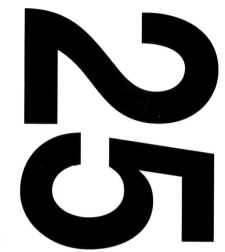

playing with others

In this chapter you will learn about:

- other opportunities for playing your guitar.

One of the most rewarding ways of making music is to be found by playing with others; either by playing duets or trios with other guitarists, or by playing chamber music, or by accompanying singers or other instrumentalists, such as violinists or flautists.

Duets and trios for guitars

There are some very attractive and easy duets and trios written for the guitar which can be tackled quite early on. They have the advantage of sounding musically richer than music of the equivalent difficulty played solo. Each player will need his own score which shows both (or all) the parts. Some duets are written for two guitarists of differing ability; the parts are marked *primo* and *secondo*, and you must first decide who is playing which part.

For your first attempts, you will find it far easier to learn your parts well before trying to put them together. You will probably find that a major difficulty at first is keeping in time together, and for this reason it is a good idea to start with a piece that has a definite and consistent rhythm, such as a waltz. You will also find it an advantage to sit so that you can see each other's face easily. When you begin a piece, one of you can indicate with a nod the last beat of the previous bar so that you can come in on the beat immediately afterwards. It is more difficult if the piece starts on an up-beat; in this case, it helps if one of you counts aloud a full bar and then the first beats in the bar of your entry. Eventually you will be able to dispense with the first bar's counting and just count the last few beats before you come in, indicating the entrance with a nod or glance. It is important that you choose a tempo that you both find easy, and that both of you have solved any technical problems beforehand.

When playing together you must remember that the music works as a whole so that you are prepared for either player to be dominant; you must be aware of how the melodic or rhythmic interest passes from player to player. You must analyse the music in just the same way as a solo work, working out the phrasing and finding the climaxes; any crescendos or diminuendos have to be expressed by both of you with the same intensity to be effective. When you have become more experienced, you will be able to respond very quickly to the other person's playing in tempo and dynamics.

One of the finest guitar duos of recent times was the husband-and-wife team Ida Presti and Alexander Lagoya. Sadly, Ida Presti's premature death robbed us of some truly great playing, but fortunately there are several of their recordings available.

Suggested music

Küffner, *40 Easy Duets* (Schotts GA).
Sor, *Easy Duets for Beginners* (Schotts GA).
Orlando Gibbons, *3 Dances*, arranged by Hector Quine (Oxford Guitar Music).
Marella, *Suite für Zwei Guitarre* (Universal Edition).
L. Call, *Trio in C, Opus 26* (Schotts GA).
Boccherini, *Famous Minuet* (Schotts GA).

Chamber music

Most chamber music is much more demanding than guitar duets or trios, both technically and musically. Apart from the technical proficiency assumed by both the composer and the other players, it is obviously far harder (if playing in a quartet or quintet) to keep aware of the goings-on of several different instruments; not only do you have to time your own entries correctly, but you also have to be sensitive to the mood and expression of the piece as a whole rather than just to your own individual part. However, it can be immensely exhilarating to play with others, especially if you are able to play regularly with the same group of people so that you get a feeling of rapport going between you.

You must be prepared to sight read fluently, as you will probably try out new pieces together. You must also be able to keep going at all costs; if you lose your place or go wrong, you must pick up your part again as quickly as possible. The easiest way to follow the music is to follow the instrument that has the melody line and bear in mind certain points where you come together, such as a modulation (key change) or a cadence.

The leader of the group (if in a string quartet or quintet, this is almost invariably the first violinist) will indicate the tempo at the beginning of each movement with a gesture. It is important to sit in a position where you can glance up at him so that he can indicate any change in tempo or dynamics.

On the whole, I find chamber music far more satisfying than concertos as the guitar is such a quiet instrument; although concerto recordings sound impressive, live performances are seldom satisfying since the guitar is so easily drowned by the orchestra.

Playing duets with another instrument can also be great fun. However, you will have to differentiate when the guitar is playing as an accompaniment to the other instrument, such as violin, and when the guitar is of equal importance. You also have to work out, with the other player, where you have to subdue one instrument in order to bring the other into prominence. If you are playing with a loud instrument like a piano, the pianist might well have to play throughout with a slightly softer tone than normal.

Suggested music

Schubert, *Quartet for Flute, Guitar, Viola and 'Cello* (Peter's Edition).
Paganini, *Quartet in D for Violin, Viola, 'Cello and Guitar* (Schotts GA).
Castelnuovo-Tedesco, *Quintet for Guitar and String Quartet* (Schotts GA).
Jacques Ibert, *Entr'acte for Flute or Violin and Guitar* (Alphonse Leduc).
Castelnuovo-Tedesco, *Fantasia for Guitar and Piano, Opus 145* (Schotts GA).

Accompaniment

Throughout its history the guitar has been used for song accompaniment. It is a very satisfying medium, as the great tonal variety of the guitar is able to facilitate the many different moods and styles of the human voice. It is also very demanding since, apart from the fact that many of the accompaniments are as difficult as a solo work, such as the Elizabethan songs of John Dowland, the player has to be completely subordinate to the singer and has to respond to him or her in such a way as to enhance his or her singing in mood, tempo and dynamics. Sometimes the guitarist has to help the singer by emphasising a melody line if he or she goes out of tune, or by making a slight hesitation if he or she is late coming in; these 'aids' had better be discreet, though, or you might find yourself out of a job! A singer might ask for a key chord to be played softly before the song; in this case, it is usual to play the first note of the melody at the top.

There is a wide variety of songs with guitar accompaniment, ranging from the beautiful lute transcriptions of the sixteenth century to the more ephemeral 'protest' songs of the twentieth century.

Suggested music

Six Tudor Songs arranged by Shipley (Schotts GA).
Six Songs arranged by John Williams (Stainer & Bell).
Songs of the Half Light by Lennox Berkley (J. & N. Chester Ltd).
Three Songs from 'Siete Canciones Popularas Espanolas' by Seguidilla Murciana.

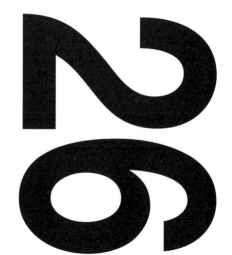

historical outline

In this chapter you will learn:

* the story of the guitar and the development of its repertoire.

Contrary to popular opinion, the guitar is not a relatively new instrument but has its roots in very ancient sources. Not only is it interesting to trace its development through history, but it also throws light on the fluctuation of its repertoire.

Together with all stringed instruments, the guitar owes its existence to the hunting bow of primitive man. The twang of the bow eventually seems to have inspired the creation of crude instruments in the shape of the lyre, the harp and the lute, which were made from wood or tortoiseshell and animal sinew. In the seventh century BC the lyre and the cithara (a larger and more sophisticated version of the lyre mounted on a large wooden soundboard) were popular instruments in Greece, and it is from the word 'cithara' that the word 'guitar' is derived. The earliest lutes, the most direct forerunner of the guitar, seem to have originated in the civilisations of Egypt and Babylonia *c.* 1000 BC. The lute was known to the Greeks as the 'pandoura' and was a very crude three-stringed instrument, although far superior to the lyre because it had a short fingerboard made of wood, giving it a much greater range of notes.

These early stringed instruments do not seem to have reached Europe until the eighth century AD, when bands of nomadic gypsies appeared throughout Europe, making a particular impression on the Latin races. In the same century the Moorish invaders brought the 'rebec', which was a primitive type of three-stringed violin played with a bow, to Spain. It became the 'popular' instrument of the people, played by street musicians and minstrels, so much so that in the thirteenth century the Church of Spain banned Roman Catholics from playing the instrument because of its frivolous image. However, the rebec had become so popular by this time that, rather than give it up, the people played it with the hand instead of a bow, thus retaining the instrument but not disobeying the Church. This instrument was gradually modified to become the mandola, and by the sixteenth century it had developed into a much more sophisticated instrument called the 'vihuela', the most popular instrument played by the Spanish aristocracy. There were three types of vihuelas:

de pendola – played with a plectrum
de arco – played with a bow
de mano – played with the hand.

By the sixteenth century, however, the vihuela de mano was the only type played. Many pieces were written for it, some of which are still in the guitar repertoire today. In 1535 the first instructional book on playing the vihuela was published, called *Libro de Musica de Vihuela intitulado El Maestro* – 'Book of music for the Hand-plucked Vihuela entitled The Teacher' – by Luis Milan, containing graded pieces for the beginner to the virtuoso player. This was followed by books by Narvaez in 1538 and finally one by Mudarra in 1546. This last book contained a marvellous collection of compositions for the vihuelist, showing what a wide range of pieces he was expected to play. Not only were there dances, such as pavanes, galliardes and fantasias, but also love songs, ballads and motets. Some were original works and some were adapted from Flemish masters like Josquin des Prés. There is no doubt that the vihuela had reached a very high artistic level, but its glory was short-lived; by the beginning of the seventeenth century the 'guittarra' had replaced the vihuela in Spain.

It is impossible to give a precise date when the guitar *per se* came into being. However, it is known that during the fourteenth century there were two instruments bearing the name 'guittarra': the 'guittarra latina' and the 'guittarra Morisca'; the former had a flat back and a single sound hole and was used for playing chords, the latter a vaulted back, several sound holes and a large fingerboard and was used for playing melodies. The 'guittarra Morisca' had disappeared from Spain by the sixteenth century, when the guitar had become the instrument of the working class, leaving the vihuela to the aristocracy. At this time the guitar had four pairs of strings, tuned to the same pitch as the inside strings of the vihuela: CFAD. In the middle of the sixteenth century another string was added and the pitch of the other strings was tuned up a tone: ADGBE. This is the tuning of the five upper strings in the guitar today.

The guitar reached England in Tudor times in the shape of the 'gittern' which was played with a plectrum and used for song accompaniment. By 1621 it had been superseded by the larger Spanish guitar, which won popularity through its stronger tone and greater versatility. By the mid-seventeenth century the guitar was being played throughout Europe. In 1627 the first instructional book on playing the Spanish guitar was published, entitled *Guittarra Espanola y Vandola*; in it the author, Dr Juan Carlos y Amat, described how to play the songs and dances of the day using a chord system on the first four frets.

By now the guitar looked similar to the present-day instrument, although it possessed only eight frets and was less 'waisted' than the modern version. These early guitars were often elaborately decorated with inlaid wood and mother-of-pearl. They had four pairs of strings tuned Aa Dd Gg Bb and a single top string, E, called a chanterelle.

A foremost guitarist of the seventeenth century was the Italian Francesco Corbetta, who was guitar-master to Louis XIV of France. During his lifetime he published several books of guitar tablature and travelled both in Europe and across the Channel to England, where he inspired Charles II to take up the instrument. Corbetta dedicated a collection of his pieces, *La Guittarre Royalle*, to Charles II, which consisted of many courtly dances such as gavottes, jigs and minuets. His pupil Robert de Visée (*c.* 1650–*c.* 1725) continued as court guitarist and also achieved fame as a composer; some of his compositions are still performed, notably the *Suite in D Minor*, which is justly famous. Gaspar Sanz (1640–1710) was guitarist to the Viceroy of Aragon and was also a famous composer of the period, though perhaps best known as the author of *Instruccion de Musica sobre la Guittarra Espanola*.

Gaspar Sanz was the last serious composer of this period to play the guitar; the harpsichord was gaining in popularity together with the violin and 'cello, particularly in Northern Europe. In Spain, however, the guitar was as popular as ever an instrument to play, but it is interesting to note that the greatest Spanish court instrumentalist of the time, Domenico Scarlatti (1685–1757), who lived and worked in Spain and Portugal for forty years, did not compose for the guitar at all, although his works are clearly influenced by it.

But although composers were turning more and more to other instruments, the guitar was still played by many people and it continued to develop in design. In the late eighteenth century a sixth string was added, tuned two octaves lower than the top E string. This is often accredited to a German instrument-maker, August Otto, although Mediterranean guitarists, inspired by the six-string vihuela, had been experimenting with six-string guitars for at least a century. At this time mid-Europe, despite an interest in the guitar as a novelty instrument, was caught up in the exciting new world of opera, symphony orchestras and, of course, the piano. The French guitar-makers at the end of the eighteenth century abandoned the double strings in favour of six single strings, since the gut strings were difficult to keep in tune with one another. For the same reason, the three bass strings were made of silk wound with silver wire, whilst the three treble strings were made of gut; this also strengthened the tone of the bass strings and added variety to the overall tone colour.

The number of frets varied from nine to seventeen, but by this time they were invariably inlaid in the fingerboard and made of brass, as opposed to the moveable frets which were tied on, as in the very early guitars. The tuning pegs were either at the side of the head of the guitar, like those of a violin, or at the back, like those of a Flamenco guitar. Inside the guitar, the belly was braced by two to five bars running transversely across it.

A final development, but one that was perhaps the most important of all, was a book published in 1799 by Fernando Ferandiere entitled *Arte de tocar la Gittarra Espanola por Musica*. This was the first instructional manual to teach the method of playing from notes rather than tablature.

The Romantic period between the late eighteenth and mid-nineteenth centuries saw great composers such as Mendelssohn, Schumann, Chopin and Liszt composing principally for the piano or orchestra. Some of these composers showed some interest in the guitar, such as Schubert, who composed many songs with guitar accompaniment; or Berlioz, who described the guitar as a miniature orchestra; or Paganini, who was almost as fine a guitarist as he was a violinist and composed quite extensively for the guitar. However, the guitar had its own exponents, including the three Italians Carulli (1770–1841), Carcassi (1792–1853) and Giuliani (1781–1829), and the Spaniards Aguado (1784–1849) and Sor (1780–1839). The most outstanding was Fernando Sor, who spent most of his life in France and also made a great impact on London Society when he made his concert début there in 1815. He wrote scores of compositions for the guitar and also a remarkable book on guitar technique called *Méthode pour la Guitare*, published in 1830. He helped to develop the structural design of the guitar by commissioning instruments made of thin, lightweight woods, and a new form of internal bracing called 'fan strutting'. This was a method (still used) of using five struts, spread like an open hand, beneath the belly of the guitar, which had the effect of distributing the vibrations of the strings, thus enriching the bass notes and enlarging the tone generally. This period began to establish the names of great guitar-makers: Torres in Spain, Panormo in London and Lacot in France.

But the guitar continued to wane in popularity during the rest of the nineteenth century and was not revived until the turn of the century with the inspired example set by the brilliant Spanish guitarist Francisco Tarrega (1854–1909). Apart from giving concerts, composing and transcribing many classical works suitable for the guitar, he was a gifted teacher and did much to establish a technique, particularly for the right hand. Through him a whole new generation of performers and composers grew up. One of his most famous pupils was Miguel Llobet, whose own circle of friends and pupils included Andres Segovia.

The twentieth-century history of the guitar is well known: its ever-increasing repertoire, including works by leading contemporary composers such as Benjamin Britten, Richard Rodney Bennett and Lennox Berkley, and, of course, the ever-increasing interest both amongst performers and amongst concert-goers. It seems that this time the guitar is here to stay.

repertoire

In this chapter you will learn:

• about music for the guitar from different places and periods.

It is always a good idea to work on three or four pieces at once. Choose music from a variety of periods and styles to broaden your technique and musicianship. Do not be overambitious, in other words do not try to play a Rodrigo concerto after three months, as the results can be very discouraging. However, it is worth having a shot at pieces that might not at first appeal to you; this applies particularly to twentieth-century music, which usually has to become familiar before its beauties and subtleties are apparent. Steer well clear of transcriptions from other instruments: not related instruments like the lute, since these transcriptions are obviously musically suitable and lie well on the fingerboard, but I have seen some appalling arrangements, such as the slow movement from Beethoven's *Moonlight Sonata* which would make the composer turn in his grave.

The sixteenth and seventeenth centuries are well represented by music of a fairly wide range of difficulty; I suggest you start by trying examples from an easy collection, such as the *Renaissance Dances*, published by Universal Edition, or *Collections of Original Guitar Pieces of the Sixteenth and Seventeenth Centuries*, published in two volumes by Schotts. You could perhaps follow these up with the *Four Easy Pieces* by John Dowland or the *Drei Leichte Stücke* by Bach, both published by Universal Edition, before attempting the more advanced works of these composers. Whenever possible, I suggest getting collected works. The Bach Lute Suites are an indispensable part of any guitarist's collection, but apart from odd movements they are for advanced players; try the *Gavotte in E* or any of the other shorter pieces published by Schotts first. Gaspar Sanz, Robert de Visée and Thomas Robinson are all very enjoyable composers, and I would particularly recommend *11 Selected Compositions* by Sanz, published by Ricordi, de Visée's *Suite in D Minor*, published by Universal Edition, and Robinson's *Allemande and Galliard*, published by Universal Edition. Frescobaldi's *Variazioni* are very well worth trying and are also easier than Bach.

The late eighteenth and early nineteenth centuries have rather a dearth in works of substance. As you should know from Chapter 26, there were several composers – Aguado, Diabelli and Carcassi, for instance – who were prolific in output. However, as these works were mainly for teaching purposes, or for entertaining ladies of leisure, they tend to be very light in content, although often quite attractive. I suggest that you try to get a collection such as those published by Ricordi: two volumes of *Compositions* by Giuliani or *19 Composiciones* of Sor. There is also an immense amount of minuets, rondos and waltzes by Sor of varying degrees of difficulty and often very attractive.

Tarrega, working in the late nineteenth and early twentieth centuries, wrote an enormous amount of estudios, scherzos and many descriptive pieces such as the *Cappriccio Arabe*. Heinrichshofens Verlag Wilhelmshaven publish a Tarrega Album edited by Luise Walker containing a wide selection of works. A contemporary of Tarrega was Albeniz. Although he composed mainly for the piano, many of his works have been very successfully transcribed to the guitar, to the composer's as well as the performer's satisfaction. Two particularly well-known examples are the *Asturias Leyenda* and *El Torre Bermeja*.

The five *Préludes* of Villa-Lobos are frequently performed and are less difficult than they sound, especially numbers 1 and 4. The *Choro Typico 1* is great fun, and the *Douze Études* are also worth trying; all these are published by Max Eschig.

The twentieth century has, of course, a glut of composers and compositions, notably the Spaniards Torroba, Turina, Tansman and Ponce; the Italian Castelnuovo-Tedesco; and, from England, Benjamin Britten, Lennox Berkley and Richard Rodney Bennett.

I have mentioned only a very few composers, but they are all representative of their period; you will soon get to know of new composers and compositions. Most publishers have lists of their guitar publications which they are willing to send, some with indications of difficulty.

glossary

All words of expression are in Italian, unless marked otherwise.

Abbreviations

Fr. = French, Ger. = German, Lat. = Latin, Sp. = Spanish.

accelerando, accel.   Gradually faster
ad libitum, ad lib. (Lat.)   At pleasure; speed and manner of playing left to performer
adagio   Slow, leisurely
affettuoso   Tenderly
affrettando   Hurrying, pressing onward
agitato   Agitated
al fine   Up to the end
alla   In the style of
allargando   Broadening out
allegretto   Moderately fast; not as fast as *Allegro*
allegro   Merry, lively, fast
amoroso   Lovingly, tenderly
andante   At a walking pace; at a moderate pace
andantino   Can mean either slightly slower or slightly faster than *Andante*
animato   Animated
apassionata   Passionately
apoyando (Sp.)   Striking
armonici, arm.   Harmonics
assai   Very
a tempo   In time again

ben marcato   Well marked

bis (Lat.)   Twice

brillante   Brilliantly

brio   Fire, vigour

calando   Gradually slower and softer

cantabile   In a singing style

capo   Beginning

con   With

crescendo
cresc. } Gradually louder

da capo, D.C.   From the beginning

dal segno   From the sign

decrescendo, decres.
diminuendo, dim. } Gradually softer

dolce   Softly, sweetly

dur (Ger.)   Major (key)

fine   The end

flagelot (Fr.)   Harmonic

forte, f.   Loud

fortissimo, ff.   Very loud

fortzato or **forzando**   Strongly accented

glissando, gliss.   Sliding

giocosa   Joyful

golpe (Sp.)   Hit

grave   Very slow, solemn

grazioso   Gracefully

largamente   Broadly

largo   Broadly, slowly

larghetto   Slowly, but less slow than *Largo*

legato   Play in a smooth, even and connected style

leggiero   Lightly, easily

lentando   Gradually slower

lento   Slow

l'istesso tempo   At the same time

ma   But

maestoso   Majestically

maggiore   Major (key)

marcato   Marked

meno mosso   Less movement

mezzo-forte   Moderately loud

mezzo-piano   Moderately soft

minore   Minor (key)

moderato   At a moderate speed

molto   Much

morendo   Dying away

non troppo   Not too much

perdendosi   Dying away

pesante   Heavily

piano, p.   Soft

pianissimo, pp.   Very softly

più   More

pizzicato, pizz.   Plucked with the thumb

poco   A little (*Poco a poco*, little by little)

ponticello   Near the bridge

presto   Quick

prestissimo   As fast as possible

pulgar (Sp.)   Thumb

rallentando, rall. ⎫
ritenuto, rit.   ⎬ Gradually slower
ritardando, rit. ⎭

scherzando   Playfully

saite (Ger.)   String

sempre   Always

senza   Without

staccato   Played in a detached manner

smorzando   Dying away

stringendo   Increasing the speed

sostenuto   Sustained

subito   Suddenly

tenuto, ten.   Held, sustained

tremolo   Trembling; rapid repetition of a note

tirando (Sp.)   Plucking

tutti   All

unghia (Sp.)   Fingernail

vivace, viv.   Lively

volto subito, V.S.   Turn over quickly

Websites

Guitarists

● Julian Bream, *My Life in Music*
www.musiconearth.co.uk/bream/indexhtm

● John Williams, *Sony Classical*
www.johnwilliamsguitar.com/

Buying a guitar

● Buy a classical guitar at GAK
www.guitarampkeyboard.com/
or
www.ebay.co.uk

● Classical guitar centre for handmade guitars
www.staffordguitar.com/

● Classical guitars by the Classical Guitar Centre Ltd UK
www.classicalguitar.co.uk/

Strings

● Shop of the world.com. Classical guitar strings.
www.shop=sotw.com/merchant2/merchant.mvc

● Classical Guitar Big String Company (USA)
www.banjostrings.com/classic.htm

Music

● Classical guitar tablature
http//alt.venus.co.uk/weed/music/classtab/

● Classical guitar tablature
http://www.newmill.com/

● Jubings free classical guitar music
www.geocities.com/jubing/

● Free guitar sheet music
www.musicaviva.com

● Midi classics guitar sequences (music library)
www.midi-classics.com/clguit.htm

● Classical guitar sheet music (music and videos)
www.chordmelody.com/newpage9.htm

● Classical guitar music
www.angelfire.com/ak/apnv

● Classical guitar repertoire guide
http//classicalguitar.freehosting.net/

● Classical guitar masterpieces
www.musicroom.com/se/io

● Classical music downloadable scores (guitar scores)
www.2.50megs.com/

General

● Classical guitar books (books and music)
www.guitarbooks.com/classical.html

● Guitar bookstore (books and music)
www.sffworld.com/pro/guitar/taclassics.html

● Ashley Mark Publishing Company (publications, videos, magazine etc.)
www.ashleymark.co.uk/

● Classical guitar (magazine)
www.ashleymark.co.uk/classicalguitar/cgcurrenthtm

● Guitar websites
www.coneguitar.com/links.html

● Classical guitar links
www.staffordguitar.com/links.html

● Guitar Vista welcome page (information and news)
www.guitarvista.com/

● UK classical guitar societies directory
www.classicalguitar.freeserve.co.uk/ukcgs.htm

● World's largest collection (classical guitar disks)
www.midisource.net/

● Classical guitar (alternative guitar clubs/music/writers)
www.theguitarprrt.com/classical

Disclaimer

The publisher has used its best endeavours to ensure that URLs for external websites referred to in this book are correct and active at the time of going to press. However, the publisher has no responsibility for the websites and can make no guarantee that a site will remain live or that the content is or will remain appropriate.

Afrikaans
Access 2002
Accounting, Basic
Alexander Technique
Algebra
Arabic
Arabic Script, Beginner's
Aromatherapy
Astronomy
Bach Flower Remedies
Beginner's Turkish
Bengali
Better Chess
Better Handwriting
Biology
Body Language
Book Keeping
Book Keeping & Accounting
Brazilian Portuguese
Bridge
Buddhism
Bulgarian
Business Studies
C++
Calculus
Cantonese
Card Games
Catalan
Chess
Chi Kung
Chinese
Chinese Script, Beginner's
Chinese, Beginner's
Christianity

Classical Music
Copywriting
Counselling
Creative Writing
Crime Fiction
Croatian
Crystal Healing
Czech
Danish
Desktop Publishing
Digital Photography
Digital Video & PC Editing
Drawing
Dream Interpretation
Dutch
Dutch Dictionary
Dutch Grammar
Dutch, Beginner's
Eastern Philosophy
ECDL
E-Commerce
Electronics
Engish Grammar as a Foreign
Language
English as a Foreign Language
English for International Business
English Grammar
English Language, Life & Culture
English Verbs
English Vocabulary
English, American, as a Foreign
Language
English, Correct
English, Instant, for German Speakers
English, Instant, for Italian Speakers
English, Instant, for Spanish Speakers
English, Teaching One to One
Ethics
Excel 2002
Feng Shui
Film Making
Film Studies
Finance for nn-Financial Managers
Finnish

Flexible Working
Flower Arranging
French
French Grammar
French Grammar, Quick Fix
French Language, Life & Culture
French Starter Kit
French Verbs
French Vocabulary
French, Beginner's
French, Instant
Gaelic
Gaelic Dictionary
Genetics
Geology
German
German Grammar
German Grammar, Quick Fix
German Language, Life & Culture
German Verbs
German Vocabulary
German, Beginner's
German, Instant
Go
Golf
Greek
Greek Script, Beginner's
Greek, Ancient
Greek, Beginner's
Greek, Instant
Greek, New Testament
Guitar
Gulf Arabic
Hand Reflexology
Hebrew, Biblical
Herbal Medicine
Hieroglyphics
Hindi
Hindi Script, Beginner's
Hindi, Beginner's
Hinduism
How to Win at Horse Racing
How to Win at Poker
HTML Publishing on the WWW

Human Anatomy & Physiology
Hungarian
Icelandic
Indian Head Massage
Indonesian
Internet, The
Irish
Islam
Italian
Italian Grammar
Italian Grammar, Quick Fix
Italian Language, Life & Culture
Italian Verbs
Italian Vocabulary
Italian, Beginner's
Italian, Instant
Japanese
Japanese Language, Life & Culture
Japanese Script, Beginner's
Japanese, Beginner's
Japanese, Instant
Java
Jewellery Making
Judaism
Korean
Latin
Latin American Spanish
Latin Dictionary
Latin Grammar
Latin, Beginner's
Letter Writing Skills
Linguistics
Mah Jong
Managing Stress
Marketing
Massage
Mathematics
Mathematics, Basic
Media Studies
Meditation
Mosaics
Music Theory
Needlecraft
Negotiating

teach yourself ®

Nepali
Norwegian
Origami
Panjabi
Persian, Modern
Philosophy
Philosophy of Mind
Philosophy of Religion
Philosophy of Science
Photography
Photoshop
Physics
Piano
Planets
Planning Your Wedding
Polish
Politics
Portuguese
Portuguese Grammar
Portuguese Language Life & Culture
Portuguese, Beginner's
Portuguese, Brazilian
Portuguese, Instant
Postmodernism
Pottery
Powerpoint 2002
Presenting for Professionals
Project Management
Psychology
Psychology, Applied
Quark Xpress
Quilting
Recruitment
Reflexology

Reiki
Relaxation
Retaining Staff
Romanian
Russian
Russian Grammar
Russian Language Life & Culture
Russian Script, Beginner's
Russian, Beginner's
Russian, Instant
Sanskrit
Screenwriting
Serbian
Setting up a Small Business
Shorthand, Pitman 2000
Sikhism
Spanish
Spanish Grammar
Spanish Grammar, Quick Fix
Spanish Language, Life & Culture
Spanish Starter Kit
Spanish Verbs
Spanish Vocabulary
Spanish, Beginner's
Spanish, Instant
Speaking on Special Occasions
Speed Reading
Statistical Research
Statistics
Swahili
Swahili
Swahili Dictionary
Swedish
Tagalog
Tai Chi
Tantric Sex
Teaching English as Foreign Language
Teams and Team-Working
Thai
Time Management
Tracing your Family History
Travel Writing
Trigonometry
Turkish

Typing
Ukrainian
Urdu
Urdu Script, Beginner's
Vietnamese
Volcanoes
Watercolour Painting
Weight Control through Diet and Exercise
Welsh
Welsh
Welsh Dictionary
Welsh Language Life & Culture
Wills and Probate
Wine Tasting
Winning at Job Interviews
Word 2002
World Faiths
Writing a Novel
Writing for Children
Writing Poetry
Xhosa
Yoga
Zen
Zulu

includes audio CD

jazz
rodney dale

- Do you want to discover the musical and cultural history of jazz?
- Do you want to understand its musical structure and the way in which it is played?
- Are you looking to improve your understanding, appreciation and enjoyment of jazz?

Jazz is an essential guide for everyone whose imagination has been captured by the exciting world of jazz. Whether you want to know about the origins and development of jazz, or about important practitioners and bands, this book does it all. The audio CD helps to enhance your listening experience with examples of jazz styles and exercises to develop your understanding further.

Rodney Dale has been involved with jazz for over 40 years, including playing piano with a number of bands, organizing classes and workshops on jazz appreciation and writing books on the subject.

includes
audio CD

piano
gillian shepheard

- Are you looking for an enjoyable introduction to the piano?
- Do you want to play from the very start?
- Would you like to improve your skills?

Piano will take you from choosing your instrument right through to playing simple music beautifully. You will easily absorb essential techniques and theory and by the last page you will have the firm foundations of a fine technique and comprehensive musicianship. It includes an integral audio CD to help you recognize the sounds you want and shows you how to achieve them.

Gillian Shepheard studied piano at the Guildhall School of Music and Drama in London. She has taught students of all ages and abilities over many years.

includes
audio CD

music theory
margaret richer

- Are you looking for a basic introduction to music?
- Do you want exercises to help you understand how it works?
- Would you like to get more out of listening to and making music?

Music Theory is the ideal book for exploring the fascinating mechanics of music. If you are a complete beginner, the clear explanations, practical activities and accompanying CD will be an ideal introduction; if you already have some knowledge, they will help you to increase your understanding and enjoyment of both playing and listening to music.

Margaret Richer studied music at Los Angeles Valley College and California State University. She has taught music theory and piano for many years.

includes
audio CD

classical music
stephen collins

- Are you new to classical music but want a comprehensive and practical introduction?
- Do you want to develop both your listening skills and knowledge of the genre?
- Do you want to gain the confidence to extend your musical experiences further?

Classical Music is a clear and concise guide that takes the listening experience as the starting point, and fills in factual details along the way. It introduces new topics step by step, and covers the architecture of music, the historical background, the instruments of the orchestra, as well as guidance on starting a collection of recorded music. The audio CD helps to enhance your listening experience with extracts from key works.

Dr Stephen Collins studied music at Liverpool and Birmingham. He has taught the subject to a wide range of students, and now works in publishing.